Social Criticism and Social Vision in Ancient Israel

Social Criticism and Social Vision in Ancient Israel

Walter Brueggemann

Edited by K. C. Hanson

CASCADE Books • Eugene, Oregon

SOCIAL CRITICISM AND SOCIAL VISION IN ANCIENT ISRAEL

Copyright © 2016 Walter Brueggemann. All rights reserved. Except for brief quotations in critical publications or reviews, no part of this book may be reproduced in any manner without prior written permission from the publisher. Write: Permissions, Wipf and Stock Publishers, 199 W. 8th Ave., Suite 3, Eugene, OR 97401.

Cascade Books
An Imprint of Wipf and Stock Publishers
199 W. 8th Ave., Suite 3
Eugene, OR 97401

www.wipfandstock.com

ISBN 13: 987-1-4982-0641-9 (paperback)
ISBN 13: 987-1-4982-0643-3 (hardcover)
ISBN 13: 987-1-4982-0642-6 (ebook)

Cataloging-in-Publication data:

Names: Brueggemann, Walter. | Hanson, K. C. (Kenneth C.).

Title: Social criticism and social vision in ancient Israel / Walter Brueggemann ; edited by K. C. Hanson.

Description: Eugene, OR: Cascade Books, 2016. | Includes bibliographical data and indexes.

Note: Essays republished in revised form from Festschriften.

Identifiers: ISBN: 987-1-4982-0641-9 (paperback) | ISBN: 987-1-4982-0643-3 (hardcover) | ISBN: 987-1-4982-0642-6 (ebook)

Subjects: LCSH: Bible. O.T.—Criticism, interpretation, etc. | Bible. Old Testament—Theology.

Classification: BS1192 B75 2016 (print). | BS1192 (ebook).

Manufactured in the U.S.A.

Contents

Abbreviations | vii
Foreword by K. C. Hanson | ix
Preface | xi

1 Social Criticism and Social Vision in the Deuteronomic
    Formula of Judges | 1

2 A Poem of Summons (Isaiah 55:1–3), a Narrative of Resistance
    (Daniel 1:1–21) | 21

3 Psalms 9–10: A Counter to Conventional Social Reality | 35

4 Prophetic Imagination towards Flourishing | 53

5 A Royal Miracle and Its *Nachleben* | 68

6 The Living Afterlife of a Dead Prophet: Words that Keep Speaking | 83

7 The Tearing of the Curtain: Matthew 27:51 | 94

8 Five Strong Rereadings of the Book of Isaiah | 99

Acknowledgments | 119
Scripture Index | 121
Name Index | 127

Abbreviations

BDB	Francis Brown, S. R. Driver, and Charles A. Briggs, *A Hebrew and English Lexicon of the Old Testament*
BHT	Beiträge zur historischen Theologie
Bib	*Biblica*
BTB	*Biblical Theology Bulletin*
BWANT	Beiträge zur Wissenschaft vom Alten und Neuen Testament
BZAW	Beihefte zur Zeitschrift für die alttestamentliche Wissenschaft
CBQ	*Catholic Biblical Quarterly*
HBT	*Horizons in Biblical Theology*
HSM	Harvard Semitic Monographs
Int	*Interpretation*
IRT	Issues in Religion and Theology
JBL	*Journal of Biblical Literature*
JNES	*Journal of Near Eastern Studies*
JSOT	*Journal for Study of the Old Testament*
JSOTSup	Journal for the Study of the Old Testament Supplement Series
JTS	*Journal of Theological Studies*
LXX	Septuagint
NRSV	New Revised Standard Version
OBT	Overtures to Biblical Theology

Abbreviations

OTL	Old Testament Library
SBLDS	Society of Biblical Literature Dissertation Series
SBLMS	Society of Biblical Literature Monograph Series
SBT	Studies in Biblical Theology
ThBü	Theologische Bücherei
ThTo	*Theology Today*
VT	*Vetus Testamentum*
VTSup	Vetus Tesamentum Supplements
WF	Wege der Forschung
WMANT	Wissenschaftliche Monographien zum Alten und Neuen Testament
ZAW	*Zeitschrift für die alttestamentliche Wissenschaft*
ZTK	*Zeitschrift für Theologie und Kirche*

Foreword

The reasons I never tire of reading Walter Brueggemann's writings are many: he doesn't confine himself to one group of biblical texts, he has a fresh take on each passage he examines, he repeatedly introduces me to other scholars' works I haven't previously encountered, and he doesn't claim to have the last word in interpretation—part of his dialogical approach. But he is also someone who can examine both the fine points of linguistic usage and yet always keep in view how this will inform a reading that illuminates the social, political, and theological aspects of the ancient writing (see especially his *A Pathway of Interpretation* [Cascade Books, 2008]).

As you read the essays contained in this volume, I hope that you will get a glimpse of not only Brueggemann's erudition, but also a sense of his humanity, his sense of humility before the text, and his engagement with our ancestors in faith.

All the essays contained here were originally published in *Festschriften*—many of them difficult to find. This is the third such volume, following *The Role of Old Testament Theology in Old Testament Interpretation: And Other Essays* (Cascade Books, 2015) and *The God of All Flesh: And Other Essays* (Cascade Books, 2015).

K. C. Hanson
Eugene, Oregon
27 July 2016

Preface

While this collection of essays ranges across various parts of the scriptural canon, at its center is my understanding of the prophetic task, an understanding that is reflected in the title given to the collection. It is evident that the themes of "judgment and hope" dominate the prophetic horizon. It is, moreover, clear that in canonical perspective that these themes of judgment and hope are deeply related to each other. Ronald Clements, from his canonical perspective, has observed: "Distinctive patterns have been imposed on the prophetic collections of the canon so that warnings of doom and disaster are always followed by promises of hope and restoration . . . [The prophetic material] acquired an overarching thematic unity. This centered on the death and rebirth of Israel, interpreted theologically as acts of divine judgment and salvation."[1] While the canonical structure delivered such an outcome that ends in promise and expectation, that outcome is not clear or assured in the specific utterance or in subsequent reading of any particular text.

My own reading of the twin themes of judgment and hope, since my early book, *The Prophetic Imagination*, is in terms of "prophetic critique" and "prophetic alternative." These terms, I intend, draw the themes of judgment and hope away from an excessively *theological* accent and into more immediate contact with the actual processes of *socio-economic political* reality. In this collection of essays, the two themes are especially clear in my essay on Psalms 9–10. There the accent of critique is accomplished by placing in the mouth of the "wicked rich" expressions of condescending self-assured autonomy. Thus they are convicted "out of their own mouth." Conversely these psalms eventually feature the urgent petition of the poor who yearn for an alternative but who can find no effective socio-economic advocate other than YHWH. Thus YHWH is by this act of rhetoric drawn into economic political reality and is voiced as an agent who will make a

---

1. Ronald E. Clements, "Patterns in the Prophetic Canon," in *Canon and Authority: Essays in Old Testament Religion and Theology*, edited by George W. Coats and Burke O. Long (Philadelphia: Fortress, 1977) 49, 53.

difference in actual social reality. The brief narrative I have considered in essay #8 exhibits the same themes in a less direct way. Here the articulation of alternative is done by the disenfranchised widow who insists on restoration. She refuses the status quo and demands her recovery of economic viability as an alternative. The critique of present unjust arrangements is implicit in her relentless petition and in the plot of the narrative itself, especially as it sits in the midst of the larger royal narrative, being quite aware that it is the kings who guarantee the unjust system against which she petitions.

It will be readily seen that both themes are spectacular dissents from a "steady state epistemology" that undergirds and supports our consumer culture. That "steady state" on the one hand assumes that there will be and can be *no serious disruption* of our technological progress that makes us increasingly safe and happy. On the other hand, it assumes that there are *no new gifts to be given* and no new visions to enacted, because steady state epistemology can allow for no agent other than that of the system. Thus the two prophetic themes are inherently subversive of status quo reality, either in the ancient world of the royal order or in our contemporary world.

The range of these essays suggests that Israel's imagination, over the centuries, was endlessly shaped by these two themes. On the one hand we have specific utterances and narrative performances. On the other hand we have wise editorial procedures that echo, treasure, and reperform the specificities. Such belated editorial practices are on exhibit in the formulae of the book of Judges and in the editorial arrangement of the books of Kings that permits the prophetic narratives to interrupt the royal chronology.

I have not often carried these themes into the New Testament. When one does so, it is clear that they are transposed into the themes of *crucifixion and resurrection* that constitute, in narrative specificity, the way in which the story of Jesus embodies and enacts the prophetic themes. Thus the one New Testament text I have considered here concerning the torn temple curtain constitutes a Friday *disruption of the old order* and *an openness to the new order* marked by Easter.

It requires no extraordinary imagination or scholarly expertise to see that these themes are urgent in our present social circumstance. It does not surprise that the performance of judgment and hope arise with effective authority, characteristically, "from below" or "from the margin." That establishment power and establishment certitude are under assault among us is not very surprising. While our National Security State, in the service

Preface

of an unsustainable consumerism, does its best to silence such voices of critique and alternative, the bet of the tradition is that such silencing finally will not be successful.

I am, as always, grateful to K. C. Hanson and his colleagues at Wipf and Stock. I am grateful as well to the roster of formidable scholars to whom these essays were initially dedicated from whom I have learned so much. And I am grateful to my several on-going conversation partners who continue to evoke within me enough courage and freedom to continue, as I am able, the joyous work of these two themes.

Walter Brueggemann
Columbia Theological Seminary

1

Social Criticism and Social Vision in the Deuteronomic Formula of the Judges[1]

The four-fold formula of the book of Judges is easily identified.[2] It has long been regarded as an identifiable mark of Deuteronomistic theology. Walter Beyerlin has reviewed the data.[3] He has subjected the materials to a careful literary analysis, indicating a possible way in which the materials have developed. It is clear from his study that the formula: a) is old and to be dated before the Deuteronomist,[4] b) that the material of the formula is not a unity, but may be treated in its constituent parts,[5] and c) that the formulation has peculiar connections with Deuteronomy 32,[6] which (following Eissfeldt and Wright)[7] may be dated early.

Two reasons make it possible to reconsider the materials of the formula in light of Beyerlin's careful analysis. First (and most important), Beyerlin's analysis is confined to issues of literary analysis and relations. Since his publication in 1963, much greater attention has been given to

---

1. This essay is offered in gratitude to Professor Wolff for the helpful way in which he has modeled the combination of evangelical passion and meticulous scholarship. It is offered with thanks for his generous attentiveness to Americans who have sojourned in Heidelberg. —The essay, of course, assumes Wolff's "The Kerygma of the Deuteronomic Historical Work."

2. The fullest treatments are those of Richter, *Traditionsgeschichtliche Untersuchungen*; and Richter, *Die Bearbeitungen des "Retterbuches."*

3. Beyerlin, "Gattung und Herkunft."

4. Ibid. 15. He has observed that some parts of the familiar, stylized language do not have close parallels in Deuteronomy (cf. ibid., 10).

5. Ibid., 2–7.

6. Ibid., 17–23.

7. Wright, "The Lawsuit of God," 36–62; Eissfeldt, "Das Lied Moses."

sociological analysis of texts.[8] That is, forms as well as substance of the texts reflect cultural interests, power arrangements, and epistemological commitments corresponding to social circumstance. It is the suggestion of this paper that a sociological analysis of the formula in the book of Judges may supplement the results of iterary analysis.

Second (and less important), Beyerlin's analysis is a contribution at a time when scholarship generally was particularly preoccupied with the constructs of amphictyony, covenant renewal, and covenant lawsuit. Each of these figures in the judgments of Beyerlin.[9] This is not to suggest that subsequent scholarship has vitiated his analysis, for the formulations of 6:8b–10 and 10:11b–14 apparently do reflect such an intention which Beyerlin sees as oral proclamations of lawsuit.[10] But it does suggest that some greater distance from those scholarly constructs may permit other discernments as well.[11]

The Four-fold Formula in Judges

Our discussion seeks to build upon the judgment of Beyerlin that the four-fold formula of the book of Judges is not a unity, but has two distinct parts.[12] Certainly by the time of Dtr they have been built into a conventional

---

8. See the summary treatment of the important work of Mendenhall and Gottwald in the *Journal for the Study of the Old Testament* 7 (1978) and the summary of the literature in Brueggemann, "Trajectories in Old Testament Literature and the Sociology of Ancient Israel." Of special importance is the proposed synthesis of Gottwald, *The Tribes of Yahweh*.

9. Beyerlin, "Gattung und Herkunft," 27–29. Beyerlin is clear that the formula in Judges is a narrative and not a lawsuit presentation, though it may derive from that form. It is now used for instruction, he argues.

10. Ibid., 27.

11. It is clear that alternatives to a lawsuit form in Deuteronomy 32 are possible. Wright's analysis ("The Lawsuit of God," 52–58) perhaps does not fully explain the remarkable shift at v. 39. It may be, as he suggests, that the speaker shifts modes. But what historical, political, or sociological realities relate to that shift? Von Rad, *Wisdom in Israel*, 295 n9, suggests an alternative placement and dating of Deuteronomy 32 that merits consideration. On the danger of patternism in the lawsuit form, see the comment of Johnson, *The Cultic Prophet and Israel's Psalmody*, 151 n2.

12. Beyerlin, "Gattung und Herkunft," 3–5. See the important comment of P. D. Hanson, *Dynamic of Transcendence*, 54–56.

unity.[13] But in order to understand the usage, we may consider the social reality which lies behind the two parts.

The first part of the formula ("do evil/anger Yahweh") consists in the elements of sin and punishment, or more specifically, apostasy and oppression.[14]

1. The formulary of "sin/apostasy" has variations. But the most common statement is a generalized phrase without specificity: "Israel did evil in the eyes of Yahweh" (Judg 2:11; 3:7, 12; 4:1; 6:1; 10:6). In three of these cases (3:12; 4:1; 6:1), this formula stands alone and is immediately followed by the responding action of Yahweh.

In the other cases, the formula is expanded in a number of variations. The fullest statement is that of 2:11–13, which appears to have later development.[15] It includes seven supplementary verbs: "serve" (Baalism), "abandon," "walk" (after other gods), "bow down," "vex," "abandon," "serve" (Baal and Ashtarot). In its present form the series of seven provides an envelope of "serve" (a), "abandon" (b), followed by three verbs with the closure, "abandon" (b'), "serve" (a'). The other fuller formula is in 10:6–7, which has the sequence "serve, abandon, not serve." In 3:6–7,[16] in addition to the two uses of "serve," the term "forget" is used, and in 6:10, "not listen."[17]

While there is surely a difference of nuance among these various terms, we can make two general observations. First, they function to interpret and give substance to the larger formula, "do evil." Second, they interpret in an

---

13. That it has become conventional is indicated in the use made of the same reasoning by Job's friends, cf. Job 5:6–16; 8:4–7; 11:6, 13–20. Cf. von Rad, *Wisdom in Israel*, 211–12. Though the points are not laid out as clearly because of the poetic idiom, the same sequence is apparent.

14. This of course is the ground for the lawsuit hypothesis applied here. The formula can be characterized in theological language (sin-punishment} or in a political idiom (apostasy-oppression).

15. See Beyerlin, "Gattung und Herkunft," 2–7; and the judgment of Smend, "Das Gesetz und die Volker," 504–6, who discerns late "nomistic" development in v. 17 and who concludes that vv. 20–22 contain late elements. Cf. Dietrich, *Prophetie und Geschichte*, 68 n6. Neither the work of Dietrich nor that of Veijola (*Die Ewige Dynastie*) bears upon our study in any decisive way.

16. There follows an extended catalogue of the gods that departs from the characteristically lean formula.

17. The statement of 8:33–35 includes a different triad: "play the harlot . . . establish (Baalberith as god) . . . not do *ḥesed* . . . ," so that it has only secondary connections to the main formula. The only other use of *znh* is in 2:17, on which see Smend, "Das Gesetz und die Völker."

intensely theological, covenantal direction. Their concern is the exclusive and intense loyalty demanded by Yahweh.

The basic formula "do evil in the eyes of Yahweh," is of course widely used by Dtr. But taken by itself, i.e., without the other elements of the formula, it is an older formula. While it surely has theological overtones, it is equally clear that it is used to maintain social order and at times social control. That is, it is not a disinterested theological formula. For the Yahweh that is displeased is always the Yahweh championed by someone. And not unexpectedly, the one who champions Yahweh (or a certain aspect of Yahweh) is a person in authority, whose authority is closely linked to Yahweh. Thus the formula is not ever without its political implication. This would not seem to be evident in Gen 38:7, 10. There is no evident ploy here for social power. But it surely is used for the defense and maintenance of social practice (levirate marriage). The issue of social power and control is more evident in Lev 10:19;[18] Num 23:27; 24:1;[19] and 32:13.[20]

We may also mention four uses which seem to be crucially placed concerning the matter of social control and political power. The first of these in 1 Sam 12:17 concerns asking for a king as evil "in the eyes of Yahweh." On critical grounds, it is not clear how this text relates to Dtr and so it may not be an independent witness to the formula. The other three are clearer. In 1 Sam 15:19 the formula is used in violation of holy war. In 2 Sam 11:27 and 12:9 the formula is used against the capricious use of royal power, insisting on the authority of the Torah against the king.[21] Thus while the formula of Judges clearly makes a theological appeal, it employs a formula that relates to the defense and maintenance of a particular form of social order.[22]

18. The formula is positive rather than negative. But the point is the same.

19. Both formulae are positive. But the fact that one man regards curse as "right" (*yšr*) and the other regards blessing as "good" (*ṭov*) suggests the political dimensions of the formula.

20. The juxtaposition of vv. 5 and 12 makes the political point. What is in the "eyes" of Moses is also in the "eyes" of Yahweh. The transcendent referent and the political authority are identical in the use of power. Such an identification is at the heart of our argument. The theological claim of the formula embodies crucial political realities.

21. Cf. 7:14. See von Rad, "The Beginnings of Historical Writing in Ancient Israel," 198–204. It is curious that this formula has been singled out as a sophisticated theological statement, whereas the parallel use in Gen 38:7, 10 would scarcely be regarded the same way. In both cases the formula is employed to insist upon and underscore a view of social reality.

22. On the social function and use of such theological formula in the service of a social order and therefore a political authority, see Berger and Luckmann, *The Social*

2. The second part of the formula concerns punishment in the form of social oppression given for violation of social order. Here the formulae are more uniform. They include: a) a theological statement: "the anger of Yahweh is kindled" (Judg 2:14, 20; 3:8; 10:7), and b) the political consequence of subjugation, "sell into the hand" (2:14; 3:8; 4:2; 10:7), or "give into the hand" (2:14; 6:1), "strengthen the enemy" (3:12). Again the variation does not seem to be important, for they point to the same reality, with the juxtaposition of theological claim and political reality.

Of these two parts, the first, dealing with the anger of Yahweh is the more interesting. It is suggested in several episodes that the anger of Yahweh is closely linked with the leadership of Moses. That is, Yahweh is angered when Moses is not obeyed (Exod 32:10, 11, 22;[23] Num 11:1, 10,[24] 33; 12:9; 32:10, 13). Four other passages seem especially important: a) Num 25:3 uses the term especially for syncretism;[25] b) 2 Sam 24:1 relates it to the census of David, i.e., the emergence of royal power; c) Isa 5:24–25 links it to the rejection of the Torah; and most important, d) Hos 8:5 uses the term in relation to the mention of kings in 8:4. It is unlikely that the institution of monarchy is rejected in principle.[26] But clearly the anger of Yahweh relates to a wrong embrace of political authority. And linked to political authority is the mention of "calves" a hint about a wrong social order.[27]

The other formula, concerning political subjugation, calls for little comment (cf. Deut 32:30; 1 Sam 12:9). There is no doubt of political

Construction of Reality, 71 and passim; and Berger, *The Sacred Canopy*, especially chaps. 1 and 2. On the political element in the formula, see the shrewd comments of McCarthy, "The Wrath of Yahweh," 100–104.

23. In v. 19, it is the anger of Moses that is kindled. Again there is nearly identification of the anger of Yahweh and the anger of his agent, Moses.

24. This verse offers a striking hint of our formula. It employs two of our phrases, "anger kindled," and "evil in the eyes of." But one is assigned to Yahweh, the other to Moses.

25. See Mendenhall, *The Tenth Generation*, 105–21, on a plausible sociological setting for the episode. He locates the crisis in terms of syncretism and the problem of legal systems. Wolff, "The Kerygma of the Yahwist," 133, 153–55, locates the episode in the traditioning process.

26. Cf. Wolff, *Hosea*, 139. The indictment is that Israel has adopted a way of political decisions antithetical to the Northern "royal ideal."

27. Perhaps the reference to "calf" links this text to that of Exodus 32. The reference to kings here and the obvious struggle for leadership in Exodus 32 indicate how our formula is related to political control and social order. In Hos 8:1–6, two members of our formula ("cry" in v. 2, as well as "anger burns" in v. 5) are used. The connections between our four-fold formula and this passage are worth pursuing. Wolff, *Hosea*, 141, suggests these are a "fixed part" in the narratives of apostasy and paraenesis.

implication. The same figure is used with reference to Egypt because of its pride (Ezek 30:12) and the Philistines because of their maltreatment of Israel (Joel 4:8).[28] With both Egypt and the Philistines, it is for acts of political and social exploitation that the "selling" is announced.

Thus it appears that the anger of Yahweh is the middle term between "evil" and "selling." It is clear that the anger of Yahweh is a way of speaking about the price assessed in the historical process for the wrong order of society and the rejection of the right ordering of society.

3. The simplest articulation of this two-membered formulation is expressed in the three statements:

> "And the people of Israel again did what was evil in the sight of Yahweh; and Yahweh strengthened Eglon the King . . . because they had done what was evil in the sight of Yahweh." (Judg 3:12)

> "And the people of Israel again did what was evil in the sight of Yahweh, after Ehud died. And Yahweh sold them . . ." (4:1–2)

> "The people of Israel did what was evil in the sight of Yahweh; and Yahweh gave them into the hand of Midian." (6:1)

In none of these is the middle term of anger used, though its presence does not change the simple structure. In these there is no embellishment, no intensification by more elaborate rhetoric. The simple formula is an expression of the teaching of the close correspondence of *deed* and *consequence*,[29] which we may characterize as one of the primary intellectual constructs of Israel.[30] These conclusions on this formula seem appropriate:

a) The two-fold formula has no necessary linkage to the other parts of the "Deuteronomic" four-fold formula of repentance and deliverance. It is independent and expresses its own teaching.

---

28. Note the use of "requite," in vv. 4, 7, a term important for the construct of "deed–consequence." Cf. Scharbert, "ŠLM im Alten Testament"; and the foundational article of Koch, "Gibt es ein Vergeltungsdogma"; see Koch, "Is There a Doctrine of Retribution."

29. Beyerlin, "Gattung und Herkunft," 3–4.

30. That construct has been especially located in wisdom materials. Cf. von Rad, *Wisdom in Israel*, 124–37, and Koch, "Gibt es ein Vergeltungsdogma," 131–40. While the construct surely has close parallels to the teaching of the wisdom teachers, we have found no close relationship to wisdom in the terminology of Judges. The closest analogy may be in Prov 3:3–4 in structure, but not in wording. The phrase, "eyes of God," is also used there, but not in a way significant for our material.

b) The action and involvement of Yahweh (either implicit or explicit) between evil and selling is evident. We are not dealing with an automatic sphere of destiny, but with a highly theologized version of retribution.[31]

c) It is doubtful if this simple formulation can be regarded as a "lawsuit," though the fuller forms of Judg 6:7–10 and 10:10b–14 may qualify. Thus the standard Judges formula is not lawsuit but a simple "deed–consequence" assertion, which means it lives in a different setting. There is no necessary connection between this formula and the lawsuits that Beyerlin has identified, though the more expanded passages permit such an interpretation.

Deed–Consequence

Our main interest is to consider the sociology of the deed–consequence teaching presented here. While attention has been given to that teaching in the sapiential materials, it can hardly be regarded as a wisdom construct. It is equally assumed and utilized in the prophets and elsewhere in the literature. Wherever it is used, the teaching reflects a well-ordered, coherent, stable social world in which rules are well established, power is properly legitimized and consequences are reasonably predictable for the honoring and dishonoring of the stable order, established rules and legitimated power. Life makes sense. This formula means both to insist on this and rely upon it.[32]

To be sure, the deed–consequence teaching can be utilized by more than one societal claim. In every case it insists on some societal claim of a positive kind. It is not used to protest an order or to declare it null and void. On the one hand, it can be used with theological intentionality about the rule of God. But as the references to Moses suggest, the rule of God is never an abstract idea. It is a rule that has historical concreteness and therefore

---

31. Obviously it makes a difference in our label if this construct is "retribution" or "deed–consequence." Cf. Reventlow, "Sein Blut komme über sein Haupt," and the response of Koch, "Der Spruch 'Sein Blut bleibe auf seinem Haupt,'" for the distinction.

32. That the construct makes life predictable is not seriously qualified by von Rad's stress on mystery in it (cf. *Wisdom in Israel*, 124–33), for the mystery presumes the linkage of deed and consequence. It only seeks to go behind it for the sake of refinement and greater understanding. The mystery is premised on the connection of deed and consequence.

political implications. On the other hand, the deed–consequence construct can also be used for any present social order, which may be legitimated by royal propaganda, justified by the use of power, and serving the interests of the ruling class. This, perhaps, is its function in the Proverbs, if not its intent.[33] It takes no subtle analysis to know that in any stable society the rule of law tends to equate the ordering of God and the ordering of the dominant class.[34] The normality presumed in the simple formula of "evil/sell" is not only an important theological claim. At the same time it is an appeal to a social, political, intellectual coherence from which some peculiarly benefited. That would seem to be the case with Job's friends who have theological affinity with the formula in the book of Judges.[35] This is not to say they act in bad faith. It is rather that the distance between the ordering of God and the ordering of the present arrangement has been collapsed and the two are identified.[36] That is likely to happen in any use of the construct of "deed and consequence."

In our formula in the book of Judges, several options lie open for its political implication.

1. If the formula is a sanction of an early community of liberation as Mendenhall argues,[37] then the formula represents tight discipline necessary to maintain the movement and resist accomodation. Clearly syncretism

---

33. Cf. Gordis, "The Social Background of Wisdom Literature"; the judicious statement of Kovacs, "Is There a Class Ethic in Proverbs?"; and Mendenhall, "The Shady Side of Wisdom."

34. Thus every theological claim has at least a temptation toward self-serving ideology. See Mannheim, *Ideology and Utopia*; and the use made of Mannheim's construct by Paul Hanson, *The Dawn of Apocalyptic* (1975). Merton, *Social Theory and Social Structure*, 114–36, helpfully distinguishes motivation and consequence, or manifest and latent function. Thus the construct of deeds–consequences, willfully or not, orders society in a certain direction. On the social function of wisdom, see Mendenhall, "The Shady Side of Wisdom."

35. Von Rad, *Wisdom in Israel*, 211, reflects on the formula handled by the friends of Job.

36. We have observed this in three cases with Moses: Exod 32:10, 19; Num 11:10; 32:5, 13.

37. Mendenhall made this suggestion in an unpublished lecture, St. Louis, Missouri, October 1976. He suggests the formula reflects the discipline of a community of liberation which has learned that any relaxation of discipline (i.e., loyalty to the social vision of Yahweh) leads to erosion and eventually reabsorption into the dominant system against which the liberated community is organized. Thus he urges that the formula reflects political experience and realism. See Gottwald, *The Tribes of Yahweh*, on the same inclination.

then has important social political implications, for it means the erosion of the liberation movement. The honoring of Yahweh is the practice of the politics of liberation. And any apostasy toward another god carries with it the dangers of oppression. The formula assumes a correlation of theological loyalty and political possibility.

2. But the formula has a different use when set in the context of monarchy. Then the formula (even if cast as a theological formula) serves to rationalize, legitimate, and justify the claims of the royal establishment. This is not the function of the formula in Judges, but the formula of "deed-consequence" in the service of the monarchy is evident in the three cases of Joab, Barzillai, and Shimei (1 Kgs 2:5–9). Two are negative and one is positive, but each is set as a consequence for a deed:

(1) Joab:	"He did, ... he murdered ...	(deed)	
	he put		
	... therefore ... do not let ..."	(consequence)	(vv. 5–6)
(2) Barzillai:	"... deal loyally ...	(consequence)	
	... because they met me with loyalty ..."	(deed)	(v. 7)
(3) Shimei:	"He cursed me ...	(deed)	
	... bring down his gray head."	(consequence)	(vv. 8–9)

There is no statement of anger or even of vengeance. The acts are for transparent reasons of state, i.e., to maintain the present order.

3. It is likely that our formula in the book of Judges is neither the early radical formula of a community of liberation, nor the self-serving formulation of the monarchy. Rather it is the delicate posturing of reform teachers who hold for a particular vision of royal reality, tightly disciplined by Torah and resistant to syncretism. As is well known, in later Dtr, both the discipline of Torah and the resistance to syncretism come to be presented as the claim of the Jerusalem temple. But that of course cannot be presented by the history as the case yet in Judges. It is plausible that the use of the formula in Judges is much more theologically radical and much less politically concrete than are the formulae in Kings. That may be because of the historical casting of the teaching in the pre-Jerusalem period. Thus this theological radicalism by the history is a counterpart for the political specificity of the later Dtr material in Kings.

The point is that the teaching of "deed–consequence," i.e., "evil/sell" is a formula in which an order holds. There is no slippage in the *nomos*.[38] It is not in doubt that consequences follow evil or good in the eyes of Yahweh nor is it in doubt that evil causes subjugation.[39] This world is reliable, predictable, coherent and has gifts to give those who will live in it. It need be explored no further. And therefore, this passionate theological conviction can be given concrete institutional expression and can be dealt with by explicit, deliberate and intentional conduct. The conduct of Israel need be neither experimental, exploratory nor precarious (cf. Deut 4:5–8; 30:11–14). It may proceed with confidence. And even when negative behavior causes negative results, there need be no puzzlement. There is still ground for confidence, for the world has not collapsed. The proponents of this theological vision undoubtedly had in mind a rather specific quid-pro-quo political, social world which could also be trusted (cf. 2 Kings 22–23).

Cry Out / Deliver

The second part of the formula of Judges is "cry out/deliver."

1. The first member of this formula is consistently "cry out" (*zaʿaq, ṣaʿaq*; Judg 3:9, 15; 4:3; 6:6–7; 10:10–14). It remains constant and is not developed. It is a plea to be delivered from oppression. In current interpretation of Dtr the term "cry out" has been understood in terms of repentance.[40] That, however, seems doubtful in its general use, or in the usage in Judges. The term may refer to a formal complaint against or a protest against injustice (Gen 4:10; 18:20; Exod 22:22; 2 Sam 13:19; Prov 21:13; Neh 5:1; Isa 5:7). When so used, it is an appeal to a higher authority against an offender. Or it may be simply a cry of desperation, hoping for deliverance (Deut 22:24,

---

38. Here I use *nomos* as social norm. Cf. Merton, *Social Theory and Social Structure*, chap. 6, in his discussion of anomie.

39. Von Rad, *Wisdom in Israel*, 129, suggests a movement from experience to doctrine. There is no doubt that our formula in the book of Judges is on the way to doctrine. But if it grows out of a genuine liberation community, it is not yet doctrine remote from experience. It may well have been experienced that departure from the radical social vision of Yahwism leads to oppression.

40. See Wolff, "Kerygma," 87–88, and cf. Janssen, *Juda in der Exilszeit*, 74–76, more generally on "Umkehr" in Dtr. Cf. Richter, *Die Bearbeitungen des "Retterbuches"*, 18–20, on *zaʿaq*. As far as I can determine, in his more general study of "Umkehr," Wolff ("Das Thema 'Umkehr' in der alttestamentllchen Prophetie") nowhere is concerned with the term *zaʿaq, ṣaʿaq*.

27; Isa 42:2). Or it may be a general outcry against an unbearable situation in which it is not a plea addressed to anyone, but it is simply an undirected grieving (Isa 14:31; 15:4; Jer 48:4, 34; 50:46; 51:54; Est 4:1).

In the uses in Judges, only in 10:10–14 is there a development. It is used in this passage in three ways. First, in v. 10 it is indeed used as repentance, but this appears to be the only such case in Judges. However, that meaning is carried not by the term itself, but by the words which follow. Second, the term is used in historical review (v. 12), to cite past acts of Yahweh's responsiveness. And then in v. 14, Israel is challenged to seek an alternative source of help which Israel rightly refuses (v. 15). In the unit of vv. 10–14 the topic is repentance, but that motif belongs to the total wording and not to the term *zaʿaq*.

On the one hand, the term refers to the deliverance from Egypt (Exod 2:23; 3:7–9; 14:10–15; 15:25; Num 20:16; Deut 26:7; Josh 24:7). The Exodus has become a paradigm for the needful call of Israel and the caring, powerful response of Yahweh. The other primary usage is in the Psalms (9:12; 22:6; 34:18; 77:2; 88:2; 142:2, 6) which concern more intimate personal matters, though the intent and the appeal is the same.

So far as I can determine, only in Jonah 3:7–8 is the term used explicitly in relation to repentance. But again that is more weight than can be placed on the term itself. The meaning of "repentance" can perhaps be deduced for the word when Israel is accused of not crying to Yahweh (Hos 7:14) or is invited to appeal to idols (Isa 57:13) or when Yahweh refuses to listen to the cry (1 Sam 8:18; Mic 3:4; Jer 11:11–12; Hab 1:2; Lam 3:8; Job 19:7; 35:9–12; Isa 46:7). But the total usage suggests a much more limited intent. The concern characteristically is limited to a situation of need and danger and an action seeking escape from it. While Yahweh may have more in mind in the call to "cry," the voice of Israel tends to focus on extrication from a situation of oppression and/or distress. The term itself implies very little in relation to the one addressed by the call.

2. The other part of this second formula is (as in the first formula we have considered) more concrete in its political intent. The term "deliver" is used in formula in Judg 2:16–17; 3:9, 15; 10:10–15. Of course, there are many other uses in the book of Judges because of the general subject matter and the easy exchange of *yašaʿ* and *šaphaṭ*. For our purposes we may focus on the thematic statement of Judg 2:16:

> Then Yahweh raised up judges, who saved them out of the power of those who plundered them.

The characteristic statement shows that the formula speaks of Yahweh as a source of political power who will liberate from another, lesser political power that oppresses.

3. In order to analyze this second half of the four-fold formula of Judges, it is important to recognize that the combined formula "cry out/save," taken by itself is an intellectual construct in Israel of primary importance for the religion of Israel.[41] To be sure there are uses of each term alone, but it is their juxtaposition that is crucial for their function here. In Judges that juxtaposition is found in Judg 3:9, 15; 10:10–12. The other formulary texts offer some variation, but these are the decisive uses.

It is clear that the construct of "cry out/save" is not originated by Dtr nor in the book of Judges. It reflects an old and fundamental claim of biblical faith, characterizing the relation between Israel as a people in need and Yahweh as the God who powerfully responds.[42] That juxtaposition is found in:

a) the Psalmic traditions of personal lament (Pss 9:13–15; 22:6;[43] 34:7, 18; 88:2; cf. Hab 1:2).

b) the various texts surrounding the Exodus (Exod 14:10–13; cf. also 2:23–25).[44] The reference of 1 Sam 9:16 refers to the Philistines and is derivative from the model of Exodus (cf. Neh 9:27–28).

c) the anecdotal report in 2 Kgs 6:26–27, which does not appear to be influenced by Dtr.

d) a negative form in Jer 11:11–12; Isa 46:7. See also the negative counterpart to our formula in Judg 12:2. These uses will be important for the argument to follow.

e) Stylized statements that are a shorthand form of the basic claim of Israel's faith. In such uses the formula has lost most of its radical dimension that belongs to its primary uses (cf. Ps 107:13, 19;[45] Neh 9:27;

---

41. Cf. Westermann, *Theologie des Alten Testaments in Grundzügen*, 147-53 (ET= *Elements of Old Testament Theology*, 167–74); Westermann, "The Role of the Lament in the Theology of the Old Testament"; and Brueggemann, "From Hurt to Joy, from Death to Life."

42. Barth, *Church Dogmatics* III/3, 267–71, urges that it is asking and petitioning that is the heart of biblical prayer.

43. The term here is *mlṭ*, but see vv. 2, 22.

44. The term *yš'* is not used but see *nṣl* in Exod 3:8.

45. Vv. 6 and 28 have the same construct, but with different terms. Cf. Ps 145:19.

2 Chr 32:20–22). In Isa 19:20 the same structure is given a curious and bold turn.

The End of the World of Nomos

The formula of "cry out/save" expresses a major intellectual construct of Israel's faith. However, the social world of faith and power that it reflects is in tension (if not antithesis) to that reflected in the construct of "evil/sell" we have already considered. This second formula of Judges is in no way relevant to the social situation of "deed–consequence" in which both theological order and political authority are clear, reliable, and well established. Indeed, this second construct of "cry out/save" reflects persons and community in a situation in which the stable ordered reliability has failed and been found wanting. Theologically we may say it is the end of the world of *nomos*.[46] There are no known modes of conduct that will produce the desired consequences. There are no assured authorities who preside over an order who keep their word.[47] To the extent that the Torah has been reduced to a "system" that can be "worked," this formula means that the Torah can no longer be relied upon to produce a world of secure blessing. It is not only that the outcome of blessing is not received, but that the system—theological and political—is now experienced as dysfunctional. This formula is a response to the very world of "deed–consequence" reflected in the first formula of "evil/sell." (Set in the context of Dtr, who uses an older formula, this suggests the inadequacy of Josiah's reform, which appeals to "deed–consequence," and it illuminates Jeremiah's rejection of newness by way of reform as inadequate.)[48]

That the formula is a theological invitation in the face of a collapsed life-world is evident in both its primary settings. We have seen that the

---

46. On the social process and significance of the collapse of *nomos*, see Berger and Luckmann, *The Social Contruction of Reality*, 119–21; Berger, *The Sacred Canopy*, 47–51; and Merton, *Social Theory and Social Structure*, chap. 6. Merton (218–19), offers a list of indicators of anomie which may illuminate Israel's rejection of an alien *nomos*. "The end of the *nomos*" may be a shattering or a liberation, depending on one's benefit from that ordering of reality.

47. Such a rejection of the system is perhaps reflected in Jeremiah's programmatic word *šqr*. Cf. Overholt, *The Threat of Falsehood*.

48. On Jeremiah's attitude toward the reform, see the old but judicious statement of Skinner, *Prophecy and Religion*, chap. 7. See the summary of Rowley, *Men of God*, 158–68; and the bibliography of Miranda, *Marx and the Bible*, 74 n37.

formula in Israel is especially linked to the Exodus event. That is, by the use of this formula, Israel moves from the epistemology and promises of Egypt to cast its lot with this other One who is always something of an unknown quantity.

The system of Egypt can be "worked," i.e., can be reduced to "deed–consequence." And as the Exodus is a departure from that system with Yahweh, so the yearning to return (Exod 16:3; Num 14:2-4) is a desire to re-enter the imperial world of "deed–consequence." The choice is between a safe world of "deeds–consequences" that crushes, and Yahweh's own version of "save" (cf. Exod 17:4-6; Num 12:13-14).

The situation is not different in the other primary use of the complaint psalm. There also the speaker has experienced the deep failure of the system. He is at a loss to make the system work. Now he must make an appeal to an alternative form of hope and help.

Let us consider the situation of those who must utilize the construct of "cry out/save." They are in distress in the Psalms, for the other systems of support and reward have failed. See the extreme statement in Job 30. Or, alternatively, they are the slaves of the Egyptian empire who look for an appeal against Pharaoh. Either way, they are those for whom the "deed–consequence" frame of reference has failed or even become hostile. And they must at some risk entrust themselves to this alternative life-world where things are much more precarious. But the alternative (if I have correctly understood the contrast of the constructs of "deed–consequence" and "cry out/save") admits of new possibility. We may thus summarize: the former formula reflects a well-ordered and predictable world of law (*nomos*). The latter is a world that relies on the freedom of Yahweh and looks to his faithful but unpredictable graciousness. This second formula breaks with the old *nomos*. Its speaker is in a *pre-nomos* situation of dangerous grace (*yṣ'*), which has both theological and political dimensions.

Our argument is that this is not simply a theological issue. It is rather a distinction between life-worlds[49] with contrasting political possibilities, epistemological commitments, and modes of certitude. Any attempt to understand the formulae theologically apart from such a political dimension misunderstands the claim and function of the formula.

---

49. See Berger, *Precarious Vision*, on the plurality and tension of life-worlds. Note especially his three-dimensional titles on "Egypt, Zion and Exodus," terms pertinent to our argument.

Social Criticism and Social Vision

In that light then, we must understand those who use "cry out/save" as a way of existence, they stand outside the managed world of "deed–consequence."

1. Such a move from the one life-world to the other recognizes that the managed world of "deed–consequence" has failed and cannot keep its promises. Thus it embodies an important critique of the "system," asserting that it cannot be trusted. Appeal to "cry out/save" is a rejection of the other mode. Thus in Exod 10:29 and 11:8 Moses wil no more appeal to that mode of existence. Such a rejection may reflect an awareness that it is weak and ineffectual, that deeds simply do not produce consequences (so Job). Or it may go deeper to see that it is not disinterested but inequitable, so that it is biased form some, against some others (thus the critique of the system of "deed–consequence" in Isa 5:20–23; Amos 5:7, 10–12; Job 9:13–23).

2. The shift of formulae from "deed–consequence" to "cry/save" is a decision to move from one court of appeal to another, to turn from the failed, now rejected authority to an alternative authority (Yahweh) who may be more responsive, more fair, more compassionate.[50]

3. The shift in formulae thus reflects a changed model of power relations. To "cry out" and look for saving implies withdrawl from the old system of "deed–consequence."[51] Thus the "cry/save" mode of reality delegitimates the world of "deed–consequence." It asserts that the system upon which Israel relies has become a source of oppression and exploitation. At different times that rejected system may be: a) the Egyptian empire, b) Israel's monarchy, c) Israel's Torah, or d) the power and claim of Babylon.

Control and Trust

Thus the four-member formula of Judges combines two contrasting intellectual constructs, that of "deed–consequence," reflecting an ordered world of stability, that of "cry/save," a daring departure on the basis of Yahweh's

---

50. Probably too much should not be made of the verb "sell" in another context. But the Yahweh of liberation (Lev 25:42) is one who does not "sell" his people. Perhaps the saving God of the "cry out/save" construct is to be contrasted with all the lords of the "deed–consequence" construct (including the Yahweh of the establishment) who "sell" their people (cf. Amos 2:6). On the juxtaposition of theological and social implications of the Jubilee, see Yoder, *The Politics of Jesus*, chap. 3.

51. Mendenhall, "The Hebrew Conquest of Palestine," has urged that the liberated community of early Israel is one that withdrew from and denied the authority of the system, and in so doing formed an alternative.

responsiveness. The two constructs had independent development and only later were formed into a unity. The one is marked by a presumption of *control*, the other by risking *trust*. We do not know when or in what way the two formulae were combined. But we conclude it was a remarkably bold and imaginative theological achievement.

1. If the formula reflects the early liberated community before the monarchy,[52] our analysis suggests the formula urges movement from the world of imperial oppression with a managed epistemology[53] to the new world of trust, freedom, and hopefully justice. The use of the entire formula summons Israel to shift from one life-world to another, with its alternative theological, epistemological, and political claims.[54]

This suggests that "repentance" as a change of life-worlds, both political and theological, is not in the third element ("cry out"), but occurs between the two systems i.e., between the second and third elements of the formula. That is, the act of "cry out" reflects a changed orientation that is already accepted. The decision has been made to take a new risk. The "cry" acknowledges not only a new authority but also a new awareness of the situation. Now it is recognized that the world of "deed–consequence" is untenably oppressive. Until that is recognized, there will be no "cry." Thus the new act of "cry" involves a) a new theological commitment, and b) new political awareness.

2. The use of the formula by Dtr may be much more radical than has been recognized. It may mean that in the late seventh century or early sixth century, this theology urged Israel to reject a mode of reality that assumed coherence and that offered a system of security. If with Cross[55] Dtr in its major part is dated before 587, it may be a radical critique of monarchy and even of the Mosaic covenant as a source of hope, when it had become a legal system to be "worked." If with Wolff[56] the formula is used in the exile, it may be a call to Israel to awaken to its true situation in which Israel has no resource except to rely on Yahweh. Either way such a summons requires a

---

52. This early placement is argued by Mendenhall on sociological grounds and is permitted by Beyerlin's literary analysis. It is not impossible that Beyerlin's lawsuit interpretation can be understood in fresh ways in terms of the sociology of withdrawal and liberation.

53. See Brueggemann, "The Epistemological Crisis of Israel's Two Histories (Jer 9:22–23)."

54. See Wijngaards, "Death and Resurrection in Covenantal Context (Hos. VI 2)."

55. Cross, *Canaanite Myth and Hebrew Epic*, chap. 10.

56. Wolff, "The Kerygma of the Deuteronomic Historical Work."

rejection of all alternative forms of loyalty and security.[57] Such a radical call may be concerned with reliance: a) on royal modes of reality, b) on Torah-centered obedience, or even c) on the seductive promises of Babylon. The shift from "deed–consequence" to "cry out/save" is indeed an expectation of a "new thing," for the "old thing" has failed (cf. Isa 43:18–19).

3. Finally we may observe that by joining the two formulae together and treating them as one "system," what was a bold attempt to place two formulae in juxtaposition has in part served to tone down and domesticate the second formula. Now the "cry out/save" formula functions in continuity with the former. Where the two systems are contrasted, they are as radically in tension as the "deed–consequence" system of Proverbs and the bold protest of Job. But when they can be brought together, they become the managed, comprehensive scheme of Job's friends. It is the tendency of every system of management to "contain" the dangers of real repentance. It is the work of every domesticated religion to make the free grace of God a part of the system. What may have begun as a bold revolutionary proposal in time becomes a new legalism against which Jeremiah, Ezekiel, Second Isaiah, and the poet of Job each must protest afresh.

The end result gives the appearance of controlled and predictable religion in the service of a well-ordered and managed political vision. That is a far cry from a risky world of surprising gifts of power in which even the spirit can rush (Judg 3:10; 6:34; 9:23; 11:29; 13:25; 14:6, 19; 15:14, 19; 1 Sam 10:6, 10; 11:6; 16:13; 18:10).

---

57. Such a political-theological summons illuminates the exclusiveness of Deut 6:5, which is programmatic for Deuteronomy. Cf. McBride, "The Yoke of the Kingdom." He casts his exposition in terms of the political and sociological dimensions of the texts. Such a radical exclusiveness, when discerned sociologically, may illuminate Jesus' call for discipleship. This is evident in his primal proclamation (Mark 1:14–15) which implies a rejection of the other kingdom and in the demand for dear choices between kingdoms, as in Matt 6:24 and Mark 8:15. On Matt 6:24, see the forthcoming book by Miranda, *Marx against the Marxists*.

Bibliography

Barth, Karl. *Church Dogmatics*, III/3: *The Doctrine of Creation*. Translated by G. W. Bromiley and R. J. Ehrlich. Edinburgh: T. & T. Clark, 1960.

Berger, Peter L. *The Precarious Vision: A Sociologist Looks at Social Fictions and Christian Faith.* Garden City, NY: Doubleday, 1961.

———. *The Sacred Canopy: Elements of a Sociological Theory of Religion.* Anchor Books. Garden City, NY: Doubleday 1969.

Berger, Peter L., and Thomas Luckmann. *The Social Construction of Reality: A Treatise in the Sociology of Knowledge.* Garden City, NY: Doubleday, 1966.

Beyerlin, Walter. "Gattung und Herkunft des Rahmens im Richterbuch." In *Tradition und Situation: Studien zur alttestamentlichen Prophetie: Artur Weiser zum 70. Geburtstag am 18.11.1963*, edited by Ernst Würthwein and Otto Kaiser, 1–29. Göttingen: Vandenhoeck & Ruprecht, 1963.

Brueggemann, Walter. "The Epistemological Crisis of Israel's Two Histories (Jer 9:22–23)." In *Israelite Wisdom: Theological and Literary Essays in Honor of Samuel Terrien*, edited by John G. Gammie et al., 85–105. Missoula, MT: Scholars, 1978. Reprinted in Walter Brueggemann, *The Role of Old Testament Theology in Old Testament Interpretation: And Other Essays*, edited by K. C. Hanson, 113–41. Eugene, OR: Cascade Books, 2015.

———. "From Hurt to Joy, from Death to Life." *Int* 28 (1974) 3–19. Reprinted in Walter Brueggemann, *The Psalms and the Life of Faith*, edited by Patrick D. Miller, 67–83. Minneapolis: Fortress, 1995.

———. "Trajectories in Old Testament Literature and the Sociology of Ancient Israel." *JBL* 98 (1979) 161–85. Reprinted in *The Bible and Liberation: Political and Social Hermeneutics*, edited by Norman K. Gottwald, 307–33. Maryknoll, NY: Orbis, 1983.

Cross, Frank Moore. *Canaanite Myth and Hebrew Epic: Essays in the History of the Religion of Israel.* Cambridge: Harvard University Press, 1973.

Dietrich, Walter. *Prophetie und Geschichte: Eine Reddaktionsgeschichtliche Untersuchung zum deuteronomistischen Geschichtswerk.* FRLANT 108. Göttingen: Vandenhoeck & Ruprecht, 1972.

Eissfeldt, Otto. *Das Lied Moses Deuteronomium 32,1–43 und das Lehrgedicht Asaphs Psalm 78 samt einer Analyse der Umgebung des Mose-Liedes.* Berichte über die Verhandlungen der Sächsichen Akademie der Wissenschaften zu Leipzig, Philologisch-historische Klasse 104/5. Berlin: Akademie, 1958.

Gordis, Robert. "The Social Background of Wisdom Literature." In *Poets, Prophets and Sages: Essays in Biblical Interpretation*, 160–97. Bloomington: Indiana University Press, 1971.

Gottwald, Norman K. *The Tribes of Yahweh: A Sociology of the Religion of Liberated Israel, 1250–1050 B.C.E.* Maryknoll, NY: Orbis, 1979. 2nd corr. ed., 1981. Reprinted, Biblical Seminar 66. Sheffield: Sheffield Academic, 1999.

Hanson, Paul D. *The Dawn of Apocalyptic: The Historical and Sociological Roots of Jewish Apocalyptic Eschatology.* Rev. ed. Philadelphia: Fortress, 1979.

———. *Dynamic Transcendence: The Correlation of Confessional Heritage and Contemporary Experience in a Biblical Model of Divine Activity.* Philadelphia: Fortress, 1978.

Janssen, Enno. *Juda in der Exilszeit: Ein Beitrag zur Frage der Entstehung des Judentums.* FRLANT 51. Göttingen: Vandenhoeck & Ruprecht, 1956.

Johnson, Aubrey R. *The Cultic Prophet and Israel's Psalmody*. Cardiff: Univesity of Wales Press, 1979.

Koch, Klaus. "Gibt es ein Vergeltungsdogma im Alten Testament?" In *Um das Prinzip der Vergeltung in Religion und Recht des Alten Testaments*, edited by Klaus Koch, 130–80. WF 125. Darmstadt: Wissenschaftliche Buchgesellschaft, 1972.

———. "Is There a Doctrine of Retribution in the Old Testament?" In *Theodicy in the Old Testament*, edited by James L. Crenshaw, 57–87. IRT 4. Philadelphia, Fortress, 1983.

———. "Der Spruch 'Sein Blut bleibe auf seinem Haupt' und die israelitische Auffassung vom vergossenen Blut." In *Um das Prinzip der Vergeltung in Religion und Recht des Alten Testaments*, ed. by Klaus Koch, 432–56. WF 125. Darmstadt: Wissenschaftliche Buchgesellschaft, 1972.

Kovacs, Brian W. "Is There a Class Ethic in Proverbs?" In *Essays in Old Testament Ethics (J. Philip Hyatt, in Memoriam)*, edited by James L. Crenshaw and John T. Willis, 173–89. New York: Ktav, 1974.

Mannheim, Karl. *Ideology and Utopia: An Introduction to the Sociology of Knowledge*. Translated by Louis Wirth and Edward Shils. International Library of Psychology, Philosophy, and Scientifiic Method. New York: Harcourt, Brace, 1936.

McBride, S. Dean. "The Yoke of the Kingdom." *Int* 27 (1973) 273–306.

McCarthy, Dennis J. "The Wrath of Yahweh and the Structural Unity of the Deuteronomistic History." In *Essays in Old Testament Ethics Ethics (J. Philip Hyatt, in Memoriam)*, edited by James L. Crenshaw and John T. Willis, 97–110. New York: Ktav, 1974.

Mendenhall, George E. "The Hebrew Conquest of Palestine." In *The Biblical Archaeologist Reader 3*, edited by Edward F. Campbell Jr. and David Noel Freedman, 100–120. Garden City, NY: Doubleday, 1970.

———. "The Shady Side of Wisdom." In *A Light unto My Path: Old Testament Studies in Honor of J. M. Myers*, ed. by Howard N. Bream et al., 319–27. Gettysburg Theological Studies 4. Philadelphia: Temple University Press, 1974.

———. *The Tenth Generation: The Origins of the Biblical Tradition*. Baltimore: Johns Hopkins University Press, 1973.

Merton, Robert King. *Social Theory and Social Structure*. Rev. ed. Glencoe, IL: Free Press, 1957.

Miranda, José P. *Marx against the Marxist: The Christian Humanism of Karl Marx*. Translated by John Drury. Maryknoll, NY: Orbis, 1980.

———. *Marx and the Bible: A Critique of the Philosophy of Oppression*. Translated by John Eagleson. 1974. Reprinted, Eugene, OR: Wipf & Stock, 2004.

Overholt, Thomas W. *The Threat of Falsehood: A Study in the Theology of the Book of Jeremiah*. SBT 2/16. Naperville, IL: Allenson, 1970.

Rad, Gerhard von. "The Beginnings of Historical Writing in Ancient Israel." In *The Problem of the Hexateuch and Other Essays*, 166–204. Translated by E. W. Trueman Dicken. London: Oliver & Boyd, 1966. Reprinted in *From Genesis to Chronicles: Explorations in Old Testament Theology*, edited by K. C. Hanson, 125–53. FCBS. Minneapolis: Fortress, 2005.

———. *Wisdom in Israel*. Translated by James Martin. Nashville: Abingdon, 1972.

Reventlow, H. Graf. "Sein Blut komme über sein Haupt." In *Um das Prinzip der Vergeltung in Religion und Recht des Alten Testaments*, ed. by Klaus Koch, 412–31. WF 125. Darmstadt: Wissenschaftliche Buchgesellschaft, 1972.

Richter, Wolfgang. *Die Bearbeitungen des "Retterbuches" in der deuteronomischen Epoche*. Bonner Biblische Beiträge 21. Bonn: Hanstein, 1964.

———. *Traditionsgeschichtliche Untersuchungen zum Richterbuch.* Bonner Biblische Beiträge 18. Bonn: Hanstein, 1963.

Rowley, H. H. *Men of God: Studies in Old Testament History and Prophecy.* London: Nelson, 1963.

Scharbert, J. "ŠLM im Alten Testament." In *Um das Prinzip der Vergeltung in Religion und Recht des Alten Testaments,* edited by Klaus Koch, 300–325. WF 125. Darmstadt: Wissenschaftliche Buchgesellschaft, 1972.

Skinner, John. *Prophecy and Religion: Studies in the Life of Jeremiah.* Cambridge: Cambridge University Press, 1922.

Smend, Rudolf. "Das Gesetz und die Volker." In *Probleme biblischer Theologie: Gerhard von Rad zum 70. Geburtstag,* edited by Hans Walter Wolff, 494–506. Munich: Kaiser, 1971.

Veijola, Timoo. *Die Ewige Dynastie: David und die Entstehung seiner Dynastie nach der deuteronomistischen Darstellung.* Annales Academiæ Scientiarum Fennicæ. Ser. B 193. Helsinki: Suomalainen Tiedeakatemia, 1975.

Westermann, Claus. *Elements of Old Testament Theology.* Translated by Douglas W. Stott. Atlanta: John Knox, 1982.

———. "The Role of the Lament in the Theology of the Old Testament." *Int* 28 (1974) 20–38.

———. *Theologie des Alten Testaments in Grundzügen.* Grundrisse zum Alten Testament 6. Göttingen: Vandenhoeck & Ruprecht, 1978.

Wijngaards, J. "Death and Resurrection in Covenantal Context (Hos. VI 2)." *VT* 17 (1967) 226–39.

Wolff, Hans Walter. *Hosea.* Translated by Gary Stansell. Hermeneia. Philadelphia: Fortress, 1974.

———. "The Kerygma of the Deuteronomic Historical Work." In *The Vitality of Old Testament Traditions,* edited by Hans Walter Wolff and Walter Brueggemann, 83–100. 2nd ed. Atlanta: John Knox, 1982. Translated from "Das Kerygma des deuteronomistischen Geschichtswerks." *ZAW* 73 (1961) 171–86. Reprinted in Wolff, *Gesammelte Studien zum Alten Testament,* 308–24. ThBü 22. Munich: Kaiser, 1964.

———. "The Kerygma of the Yahwist." *Int* 20 (1966) 131–58. Reprinted in *The Vitality of Old Testament Traditions,* by Hans Walter Wolff and Walter Brueggemann, 41–82. 2nd ed. Atlanta: John Knox, 1982.

———. "Das Thema 'Umkehr' in der alttestamentllchen Prophetie." *ZTK* 48 (1951) 129–48. Reprinted in *Gesammelte Studien zum Alten Testament,* 130–50. ThBü 22. Munich: Kaiser, 1964.

Wright, G. Ernest. "The Lawsuit of God: A Form-Critical Study of Deuteronomy 32." In *Israel's Prophetic Heritage: Essays in Honor of James Muilenburg,* edited by Bernhard W. Anderson and Walter Harrelson, 26–67. New York: Harper, 1962.

Yoder, John Howard. *The Politics of Jesus: Vicit Agnus Noster.* Grand Rapids: Eerdmans, 1972. 2nd ed., 1994.

2

A Poem of Summons (Isa 55:1–3), A Narrative of Resistance (Dan 1:1–21)

It is a delight to offer this essay to Professor Westerman with warm and hearty thanks. My gratitude is not only for his scholarship, which is decisive for my work, but also for his gracious and generous receptivity to the host of North Americans who have gone to study with him. He has been endlessly patient and thoughtful.

The poetry of Isaiah 40–55 is enormously generative for Israel's future.[1] That visionary poetry generated powerful religious hope and political courage for the life of Israel after 540 BCE. That poetry also evoked subsequent texts, the clearest case being the text of Isaiah 56–66. Thus Blenkinsopp can assert that "passages in Is. 56–66 can be shown to relate to passages in Is. 40–55 as commentary to text."[2] In this paper I wish to investigate a different example of "commentary to text," in Daniel 1 as a midrashic commentary on the text of Isa 55:1–3.[3]

---

1. See the summary comment of Paul Hanson, "Israelite Religion in the Early Postexilic Period," 501–3. The evocative power of Deutero-Isaiah operates literarily and theologically, even if we proceed with a canonical understanding of the book of Isaiah. The current discussion about canonical criticism does not affect our present argument.

2. Blenkinsopp, "Second Isaiah," 95.

3. On the midrashic character of the Daniel narratives, see LaCocque, *Daniel*, 1–2. See also von Rad, *Old Testament Theology*, 2:313–15. On the more general interpretive practice of midrash, see Fishbane, *Biblical Interpretation of Ancient Israel*; Seeligmann, "Voraussetzungen der Midraschexegese"; and Neusner, *Midrash as Literature*; Neusner, *What Is Midrash?* has also provided a convenient introduction to and definition of midrashic study. The clearest, succinct statement concerning this mode of interpretation is offered by Fishbane, "Inner Biblical Exegesis." Fishbane (36) concludes: "The most characteristic feature of the Jewish imagination, the interpretation and rewriting of sacred texts, thus has its origin in the occasional, unsystematized instances of exegesis embedded in the Hebrew Bible, examples of which it has been my effort to recall."

A Poem of Summons

The text of Isa 55:1–3, part of the conclusion of the poetry of Isaiah 40–55, issues a summons that is in fact a promise. The summons is expressed in an extended series of imperatives dominated by the verb "come":

> come ... come ... buy ... eat ...
> come ... buy ... (v. 1)
> hearken ... eat ... delight ... (v. 2)
> incline ... come ... hear (v. 3)

This massive imperative assault suggests urgency and presses the listening community to an immediate and crucial decision.

The decision urged is to abandon sources of nourishment and sustenance that do not feed or satisfy (v. 2ab). The questions in v. 2 function as disputational speech intended to dismiss the negative option now to be rejected. The main rhetorical force of the poetic lines, however, is in the series of positive imperatives that frame the questions of v. 2. These imperatives present to the listeners an alternative that will indeed nourish and satisfy.

The promissory character of the summons is clear in v. 3b. After the three imperatives of v. 3 (incline, come, hear), the promised possibility is that your *nefesh* will live. The *nefesh* of Israel (singular noun, plural pronoun) is in jeopardy from starvation; now a freely given alternative is possible. This progrommatic promise is then extrapolated in two phrases that express the main concern of the entire poetic piece: a) God offers an "everlasting covenant," one not abrogated even by the reality of exile; and b) God asserts "steadfast sure love for David."[4] That is, the promise that "your *nefeš*" will live is interpreted to refer to God's continuing covenantal loyalty and attentiveness in a situation of enormous threat and discontinuity. It is the covenant solidarity of Yahweh that makes life possible for Israel, life that is not possible while Israel spends its money, energy, and loyalty for that which is not bread and that which does not satisfy.

---

4. On the reformulation of the Davidic promise in this text, see Eissfeldt, "Promises of Grace." My argument in this paper concerns the claim that Daniel 1 appeals to the "old text" of Isa 55:1–3; here it is clear that Isa 55:1–3 also appeals to an older text of Davidic theology (such as 2 Samuel 7). It offers a reinterpretation of that earlier text as Daniel 1 subsequently offers a reinterpretation of the poetic rendering in Isaiah 55. Fishbane, *Inner Biblical Exegesis*, 20, suggests that the "foundation text [may be] already an interpreted document." In our case, Isa 55:1–3 is already interpreted from the older Davidic materials but is again reinterpreted in Daniel 1.

A Poem of Summons, a Narrative of Resistance

In recent commentary on this passage, scholarly attention has primarily been given to the identification of the voice and genre of the summons. We may identify the following hypotheses concerning the identity of the voice of summons:

a) Begrich has offered the dominant hypothesis, followed by many scholars, that this is the summons of "Dame W Wisdom the summons as the voice of a vendor in the marketplace offering a sale to a prospective buyer.[5] As is characteristic of Westermann, he finds the antecedents in the daily life of the community. This hypothesis is a variation of an older hypothesis of Dellitzsch that this is the voice of a "water seller."[6]

d) Clifford has recently suggested, utilizing Ugaritic parallels, that the summons is the presence of God in the temple, "proximity to the deity in the deity's shrine."[7]

e) A more theological interpretation, as for example in Calvin, suggests that the summons of the poem is a summons to the Gospel, which may in Christian interpretation be given a Christological or eschatological accent.[8]

1. The hypotheses we have mentioned identify the "voice of summons" either in terms of generic interest (wisdom, vendor) or as a theological generalization (cultic proximity, royal banquet, the gospel). Neither such a literary antecedent nor a theological generalization, however, would seem to touch the unmistakable urgency expressed in the series of imperatives. This is indeed an immediate, life-and-death decision. The identification of the voice should not lead us away from the textual moment given us. The voice in the text is not that of a generic vendor nor of undifferentiated wisdom, but a pastoral poet addressing real people in a crucial moment. The summons is not just to cultic presence but to a more hazardous and more marvelous option concerning food, sustenance, and life. The real-life

---

5. Westermann, *Isaiah 40–66*, 282–83.
6. Delitzsch, *Isaiah II*, 325.
7. Clifford, "Isaiah 55," 27–35.
8. Calvin, *Isaiah*, 155–57. Calvin recognizes that "water, milk, wine, bread" are metaphors that include "all that is necessary for spiritual life." Moreover, the "metaphors are borrowed from those kind of food which are in daily use amongst us. As we are nourished by 'bread, wine, milk, and water,' so in like manner let us know that our souls are fed and supported by the doctrine of the Gospel, the Holy Spirit, and other gifts of Christ."

situation of the poem is in the midst of an empire where newness is being enacted (cf. Isa 43:18–19), and where that newness is being resisted (45:9–13). Thus we are obligated to listen more closely to the text itself than these several hypotheses permit us to do.

2. In identifying the voice of summons, by way of literary antecedent or theological generalization, scholars have not paid much attention to the negative force of v. 2. That verse issues two questions that are in fact accusations. The negative force of "not bread," "not satisfy" is central. That negative, however, is almost skipped over by scholars in their zeal to get to the positive religious affirmation. Muilenburg notes a general accommodation to Babylonian surroundings, but along with other scholars, soft-pedals the costly and total change that is called for.[9] The negative alternative here rejected, I submit, is the entire imperial world of Babylon, which cannot keep its promises, and cannot give life. The negative rejected by this poetic voice is Babylonian religion, which makes an offer of life that it cannot keep. The Jews addressed by this poet are situated in Babylon and are called to reject and deny the best religious promises offered by Babylonian religion, and with them, the legitimacy, safety, and stability that is available in the empire.[10]

3. A little at a time, we are learning to ask socio-political questions of texts.[11] In recent discussion of this text, almost no attention has been given to the socio-political dimension of Israel's faith and life in exile. Clearly the Babylonian religion critiqued by the poet did not exist in a vacuum, but was linked to and legitimated Babylonian socio-economic and political definitions of reality and organization of power.[12] Westermann has noted that the reference to bread and milk means that a split of spirit and material

---

9. Muilenburg, "Isaiah," 644.

10. The poetry of Deutero-Isaiah maintains a constant and harsh critique of the religious enterprise of the Babylonian empire. This is evident in the disputation speeches of 41:1–5, 21–29, and in the mock song of chapter 46. The lyrical dismissal of Babylonian religious legitimacy is essential to the hberation of Jewish imagination for the sake of homecoming.

11. The decisive contribution thus far has been the work of Norman K. Gottwald. Jobling, "Sociological and Literary Approaches to the Bible," 85–93, has offered a discerning critique of Gottwald's work and has identified the most important contributions of Gottwald. For a concrete example of a socio-political reading of the text that bears upon our discussion, see Goldingay, "The Stories of Daniel."

12. On the connection between theological and socio-political dimensions of Israel's textual tradition, see Hendel, "Social Origins"; and Brueggemann, "Old Testament Theology as a Particular Conversation."

is not permitted.[13] That refusal to "split" must be taken more seriously in interpretation. It means that the critique made by this urgent, imperative poetic voice is not only a theological summons, but also a socio-political one. It is not only a summons away from Babylonian theological loyalty and an invitation to the covenant of Yahweh; it is also a summons away from Babylonian socio-economic and political reality and an invitation to the historical possibility of Yahwism, which is the socio-economic and political restoration of Judah.

Thus the summons in Isa 55:1–3 is a summons to wholesale resistance to Babylonian options, both religious and political. That imperial option, both religious and political, must be resisted in all its parts because it robs exiled Israel of hope and finally of identity (i.e. *nefeš*) . It numbs Israel's imagination and robs Israel of its chance for life. Babylon is to be resisted because it will destroy the *nefeš* of Israel. The poetry invites Israel to say "no" to every form of Babylonian nourishment that denies every Jewish possibility of life. Scholarly preoccupations with antecedents and generalization have largely led us away from the concrete and urgent issue of resistance present in the text, resistance necessary for the liberation of the community of Yahweh.

A Narrative of Resistance

The story of Daniel 1, I propose, is a narrative rendition of the summons and promises of Isa 55:1–3. It is a tale of resistance (thus enacting the summons of the poem) and of success (thus receiving and exhibiting the promise of life offered in the poem).

The story of Daniel 1 moves from seduction through resistance to liberated success in three scenes. The action is dated in the narrative with reference to Nebuchadnezzar, the end of whose regime Deutero-Isaiah celebrates (cf. Dan 1:1–2).

At the outset of the narrative, we are given a glimpse of the royal, imperial context of exilic Jewish life (Scene 1, vv. 3–7). The entire scene happens, because "the king commanded" (v. 3). There is no counter-voice, no uncertainty, no hesitation. There is only one decisive voice. It is the voice of Nebuchadnezzar.

The narrative quickly lays out the three important dimensions of the plot: a) The recruits for royal civil service are to be Judahite youths who are

---

13. Westermann, *Isaiah 40–66*, 282–83.

in every way "competent" (vv. 3–4). This royal commission evokes the crisis of the narrative. b) The youths selected are to be inducted into the knowledge, skills, and intelligence of the empire, i.e. "the letters and language of the Chaldeans" (v. 4). Clearly their Jewishness is to be radically subordinated to the claims and interests of the empire. c) The Judahite recruits are to be nourished on the rich food of Babylon, perhaps as a reward, but more obviously in order to make them acceptable physical specimens for standing before the king (v. 5). They are to be chosen in the first instance because they are already handsome and without blemish; nonetheless, rich imperial food will make them more so.

The scene is one of imperial seduction, in which Judahite youths are pressed into a service that contradicts their Jewishness. In this seduction, however, there is no bad faith on the part of the king. It is assumed that any Judahite boy will be responsive to the opportunity of upward mobility into the court. The king who commands perceives his order as no threat to being Judahite, as being a Judahite is not a factor on his horizon. There is nonetheless subtle irony in the awareness that the king who would never acknowledge being a Judahite as a factor nonetheless singles out Judahites for his service. The narrator offers no comment on this odd fact, but only reports to us the royal action.

The royal seduction evokes Judahite resistance (Scene 2, vv. 8–17). Daniel is clearly the subject and champion of the narrative. Daniel understands immediately what in fact is happening. The invitation to training and service in scene 1 is presented in the narrative as a neutral, "innocent" offer. Only a discerning, faithful Jew can notice that the offer of such imperial food, given to qualify for the king's presence, is in fact "defilement." Daniel introduces into the narrative a partisan Jewish notion that would have been a surprise to Nebuchadnezzar and no doubt to the contemporaries of the narrator to whom the narrative is addressed.[14] What is offered by Nebuchadnezzar is simply "rich food" and "wine." What is refused by Daniel, however, is imperial "defilement."

---

14. This literature bespeaks the "sectarian strategy" that Stanley Hauerwas has lately championed. Of the strategy of the book of Daniel, Schwartz writes: "Well, how do such exiles manage? By dreaming, they serve their masters in good faith, with their special kind of divided integrity—a contradiction in terms. Certain things, things of the spirit, they do not, cannot promise. What they hate most of all is coercion. The flesh they permit to be coerced, but not the spirit. What they believe, they cling to with fortitude, and with an earthly tenacity that both saps their strength and replenishes it. They will not worship false or frivolous gods, for then they would no longer be who they are . . ."; Schwartz, "Daniel," 420–21,

A Poem of Summons, a Narrative of Resistance

Daniel is politically shrewd, cooperative, and discerning; all his deftness, however, is in the service of his foundational theological commitment which lies outside the empire. Thus while the chief of the eunuchs and the steward are cooperative with Daniel, we are told early that "God gave Daniel favor and compassion" (v. 9). In the first scene, only Nebuchadnezzar acts. In scene 2, the scene of Judahite resistance, God is the decisive, albeit unseen, actor who in fact dispatches the imperial officers to do his work. Daniel's courageous resolve is implemented to provide safeguards for frightened royal officers; these functionaries of Nebuchadnezzar do not understand that one other than Nebuchadnezzar in fact dispatches them in this narrative. Thus there is nothing excessively abrupt or disruptive in Daniel's resistance. It takes place inside the structures and procedures of the royal design. His action is resistance nonetheless.

Daniel's alternative to the rich food and wine of the empire is vegetables and water (v. 12). The preliminary test of the alternative program, made to reassure the royal functionaries, is effective (vv. 14–16). The Judahite boys on the lean, non-defiling diet are "better in appearance" and "fatter in flesh." The lean Jewish diet of defiance works better than the rich imperial diet.

The culmination of *liberated success* is a vindication of Daniel's firm resolve (Scene 3, vv. 18–21). Nebuchadnezzar had determined scene 1 and was completely absent in scene 2. Now the king reappears in the narrative to give the crucial verdict in scene 3. The verdict given by the king surprises no one. It does not surprise Daniel, man of faith. It does not surprise the royal officers who had already had a preview. Moreover, the verdict does not surprise Nebuchadnezzar, who is innocent of Daniel's faith and Daniel's stratagem. In every regard, Daniel and his friends are "ten times better" (v. 20). No wonder Daniel is ensconced in royal service for a long time to come (v. 21)!

Note the reticence of the narrative in telling the tale. Yahweh was not present in scene 1, which belongs completely to Nebuchadnezzar. Yahweh is decisive in scene 2, but unseen and unacknowledged by the characters. In scene 3, Yahweh is again invisible, not even mentioned in the narrative. Any external observer might have perceived Nebuchadnezzar controlling matters on his own terms. The narrator does not tell us otherwise. He does not explicitly challenge Nebuchadnezzar's dominance in the third scene. We are left to draw the conclusion that God's favor and compassion, explicit only in vv. 9 and 17, in fact not only govern scene 2, but also determine the outcome of scene 3. Nebuchadnezzar had imagined scene 3 to be his triumphant scene, but the listener moves to a very different conclusion.

Daniel is offered to the listeners of the story as a model for resistance.[15] His is a fine and careful blend of cooperation and resistance. He does, however, with discipline and integrity know where to draw the line for Jewishness (i.e., trust in God's favor and compassion) and against imperial "defilement." Notice how Daniel has drawn this line. He has refused to labor for that which is not bread, for that which does not satisfy. He has taken food and water without imperial price tags attached.[16] He has delighted his life in fatness. He has cast himself on the faithfulness of Yahweh, relying on the "steadfast, sure love" of Yahweh. He has indeed accepted the summons of the poem of Isa 55:1-3, and received its promise of life. He has received life and avoided the defilement of submitting his Jewishness to imperial domination. The summons is honored. The promise is kept.

Inner-Biblical Interpretation

I propose that the interrelation of Isa 55:1-3 and Dan 1:1-21 is that of text and commentary. The text of Isa 55:1-3, according to critical consensus, is securely dated and located at the end of the exile, at the demise of the Babylonian hegemony. The poetry of Isaiah 40-55 asserts the freedom and capacity of Judahites to depart the empire. Israel's invitation and authorization to leave the empire, while reflecting changed political realities, are cast by the poet as a theological issue concerning Yahweh's sovereignty over Babylon. That claim of sovereignty is asserted by the poet and calls for a decision on the part of listening Israel. The poet presents the large and dangerous theological decision for Yahweh's sovereignty as an act of concrete resistance to the seductive nurture of the empire. The large theological act of departure depends on the specificity of daily food.

Growing scholarly attention to "inner-biblical" interpretation permits us to understand both of these texts in fresh ways. Historical-critical study has been concerned to place each text firmly in its context of origin.

---

15. See Humphreys, "Life-Style," 217-23. See the splendid analysis of Daniel 1 by Towner, *Daniel*, 285-98. Note as well his reference to Joyce Baldwin on p. 293.

16. Moltmann, *Theology and Joy*, 54, writes of this verse: "'It's all *for nothing* anyway,' says the nihilist and falls into despair. 'It's really all *for nothing*,' says the believer, rejoicing in the grace which he can have for nothing, and hoping for a new world in which all is available and may be had for nothing." The contrasting perspectives on "for nothing" bespeak the faith of the community and the despair of the empire.

A Poem of Summons, a Narrative of Resistance

Concerning the narratives of Daniel, historical criticism has given its primary energy to the placement of the narratives in the Maccabean crisis of the second century, far away from the sixth century when its reported events purportedly happened. The result of such an historical-critical interest has been to downplay the powerful symbolism of "Nebuchadnezzar" and "Babylon" in the Daniel text. Moreover the socio-theological issues addressed in the text concerning displacement, oppression, resistance have been neglected, and affirmative and theological alternative and political possibility have been unnoticed. That is, historical criticism distracted interpretation from noticing the main theological and socio-political issues in the text.

Once it is recognized, however, that both the poem of Isaiah 55 and the narrative of Daniel 1 address issues of resistance and alternative, the two texts may be related to each other in ways not allowed by pure historical criticism. Without denying that the narrative of Daniel 1 may be much later than the poem of Isaiah 55, it is cogent to see the close connection between poem and narrative as text and commentary. This connection does not necessarily draw the Daniel narrative into the sixth century, but it does draw both texts into the typological issues of resistance and alternative that repeatedly concerned the community of early Judaism.

The move from historical-critical to "inner-biblical exegesis" permits connections between texts that we may term "midrashic." Such connections are not precise according to the measures of historical criticism. They may be much more impressionistic, reflecting enormous interpretative freedom and imagination. The identification of such imaginative connections, however, permits us to see afresh not only the "new text" derived from the foundational text, but also to see the foundational text in new configuration.[17]

Concerning Daniel, Gammie has explored these matters in most detail, but as far as I can note, he has not suggested the specific connection that is here discussed.[18] Following Gammie, Towner concludes, "We seem to be on safe ground in asserting that one function of the stories of Daniel

---

17. A basic study in this regard is that of Paul Hanson, *The Dawn of Apocalyptic*. Hanson does not carry his work as far as the literature of Daniel. He has, however, shown how Deutero-Isaiah stands at the beginning of a literary-theological trajectory that continues to develop and generate new literature and new modes of literature.

18. Gammie, "On the Intention and Sources of Daniel 1–VII."

1–6 is to assure Jews that the visionary hopes and promises of Isaiah 40–55 are indeed capable of realization among the obedient and wise of Israel."[19]

Once we have opened the possibility that the poem of Isa 55:1–3 may receive daring rearticulation and reappropriation into new contexts,[20] it is not difficult to identify some of the connections between our two texts. In these several connections, then, I suggest that the interpreting tradition of Daniel took up the text of Isa 55:1–3, which urges resistance in a Babylonian situation, and reinterpreted it for the sake of Judeans under assault in the Maccabean context. The connections between the two texts include the following:

1. The commonality of *the wisdom motif* may indeed be present in both texts, given the hypothesis of Begrich concerning Isa 55:1–3. Daniel is clearly offered as a model wisdom figure.[21] Inside the story Daniel is presented as a wise character; and the narrative itself champions wisdom as a mode of life. If Begrich is right, the summons in Isa 55:1–3 is the voice of wisdom, summoning Israel precisely to the kind of action undertaken by Daniel. Wisdom then is the capacity to discern the true character of one's context as a place where death threatens, where life is offered, and where Yahweh can be trusted to give life. Foolishness is to seek life from other sources which can only yield death (cf. Prov 8:32–36).[22]

2. The *Babylonian connection* is central in both texts, though that reference need not be read historically, i.e., as a sixth century reality. "Babylon" can be taken dramatically and metaphorically as an option for life which is clearly false and which will rob one of one's *nefesh*. Taken dramatically and metaphorically, of course, there is no impediment in reidentifying Nebuchadnezzar as Antiochus, as the oppressed community presumably

---

19. Towner, *Daniel*, 27. Von Rad, *Old Testament Theology*, 2:314 n29, suggests that parts of Daniel might be described as a *pesher* on Isaiah. See also LaCocque, *Daniel*, 1 n1, where the same judgment is expressed. On the relation of these literary traditions, Baltzer, "Liberation from Debt Slavery," 480, concludes: "It has often been observed how vague the details regarding the situation of the exiles are in Second Isaiah. About this subject we learn a great deal more from a line of literature running from Jeremiah 29 through the book of Ezekiel to Daniel 1–6. These are texts describing captivity in Second Isaiah."

20. On the reinterpretative process in relation to Daniel, see Childs, *Introduction to the Old Testament as Scripture*, 618–22.

21. Humphreys, "A Life-Style for Diaspora," has shown not only the wisdom intent of the narrative, but has shown how the wise walk a fine line between accommodation and defiance.

22. On wisdom's gift of life, see Murphy, "The Kerygma of Proverbs," 3–14.

did.²³ However construed, the figure of Nebuchadnezzar and the presence of Babylon are necessary to provide a foil for the invitation and offer of Yahweh.

3. More obvious than the function of wisdom and the cruciality of Babylon in both texts is *the concreteness of food* in both texts. "Food" here may be taken metaphorically as referring to much more than the diet of harassed Judahites. It should not however be spiritualized away from the concreteness of nourishment and sustenance. Food is a metaphor that does not lose its concrete vehicle. It does indeed refer to sustenance, life-support, and livelihood that the empire would gladly give, but at great price. The price for such food and wine is the cost of one's *nefeš*.²⁴ To spiritualize the alternative food of the poem, as commentators are prone to do, is to diminish the concrete danger and the daily urgency of the choice offered. To be sure, the food in the Daniel narrative cannot so easily be treated as metaphor as in the Isaiah poem. Nonetheless both texts address real life issues fraught with danger and risk, concerning both the possibility of historical survival and the survival of faith, freedom, hope, and imagination.

4. The common elements of wisdom, Babylon, and food lead us to see that both texts concern resistance, what Towner calls "this magnificent refusal."²⁵ The two texts belong to a sustained concern in post-exilic Judaism that the community of faith must intentionally resist being bought off and seduced, when it is offered life on terms other than the covenantal offer of Yahweh.²⁶ The issue of resistance and alternative, so crucial to the char-

---

23. Towner, "Were the English Puritans 'The Saints of the Most High'?," has shrewdly explicated the way in which these historical names become ciphers to be filled with various interpretative identities. Towner, "Daniel 1 in the Context of Canon," 291, suggests that Daniel 1 is a "refraction" of 2 Kgs 25:30. If this is plausible, the narrative is drawn more closely into the Babylonian crisis of the sixth century that preoccupied the poet of Isaiah 55.

24. In both these texts, Babylonian food robs Israel of its *nefesh*. This is an oddly telling notion, because in other contexts, it is food that restores one's *nafas*; cf. 2 Sam 16:14. See Wolff, *Old Testament Anthropology*, 10–22.

25. Towner, *Daniel*, 23.

26. Gammie, "The Classification," has demonstrated that the literature of Daniel cannot be linked exclusively to the Maccabean crisis. Thus it is the socio-theological situation of exile rather than a concrete historical placement that is important for reading the text. Schwartz, "Daniel," 424, observes, "In truth, as unearthed by research and archaeology and linguistic analysis, the author of Daniel was of another, later time, another place, and obsessed with other events entirely. He was indulging in a clever and now familiar tactic, using the Babylonian exile to illuminate the destiny of Israel in his own way . . ." Just as the pre-critical link to the sixth century is not defensible, so the critical link to the

acter of Judaism, is focused precisely in the recognition that the "alternative food" is indeed real food, even while it alludes to much more. Said in other language, resistance to the empire requires a theological-spiritual decision, but also a concrete, intentional political act. The narrative of Daniel 1, perhaps many generations after the poem, asserts and attests that the poem of Isaiah 55 is true. Life reliant on alternative sustenance is embraceable, liveable, albeit with risk. Only with this risk can there be homecoming for the exiles. Indeed, only with this risk can there be a community counter to the empire.

Conclusion

Professor Westermann has worked incessantly to clarify matters of scholarly method with particular reference to form criticism. This essay evidences in a small detail the way in which new methods are developing from Westermann's magisterial work in form analysis. On the one hand, the connection I have proposed between the two texts depends on the traditioning process of constant reinterpretation, so that texts are endlessly commentaries on earlier texts. Thus inter-textual reading has emerged as a new methodological possibility. On the other hand, the posing of socio-political questions (inchoate in Westermann's work) leads us to focus on futures generated by the text.

The heuristic value of seeing these two texts as "text and commentary" is not only to show that the narrative of Daniel 1 is not a "new text," but an old poem rearticulated. It is also to show that the poem of Isa 55:1–3 is not only a marvelous offer, but an invitation to resistance. The homecoming offered here, so crucial to Judaism, is at an enormous cost.[27] It matters therefore that the voice of summons and promise (that shows up hiddenly in Dan 1:9) is indeed the voice of the faithful God of Israel. This voice which sounds variously like a vendor, like wisdom, like an invitation to the shrine or to a royal banquet, is the voice of the God who orders wisdom, governs empires, manages alternative diets, and sustains a community of faithful obedience.

---

second century need not be held too closely. What counts is the social paradigm and the task of reinterpretation.

27. On the paradigmatic significance of exile and homecoming for Jewish faith, see Neusner, *Understanding Seeking Faith*, 115–49. Neusner has shown how the language of crucifixion and resurrection has served Jewish speech about exile and homecoming.

Bibliography

Baltzer, Klaus. "Liberation from Debt Slavery after the Exile in Second Isaiah and Nehemiah." In *Ancient Israelite Religion: Essays in Honor of Frank Moore Cross*, edited by Patrick D. Miller et al., 477–84. Philadelphia: Fortress, 1987.

Begrich, Joachim. *Studien zu Deuterojesaja*. ThBü 20. Munich: Kaiser, 1969.

Blenkinsopp, Joseph. "Second Isaiah—Prophet of Universalism." *JSOT* 41 (1988) 83–103.

Brueggemann, Walter. "Old Testament Theology as a Particular Conversation: Adjudication of Israel's Socio-Theological Alternatives." *Theological Digest* 32 (1985) 303–25.

Calvin, John. *Commentary on the Book of Prophet Isaiah*. 4 vols. Translated by William Pringle. 1850. Reprinted, Grand Rapids: Eerdmans, 1979.

Childs, Brevard S. *Introduction to the Old Testament as Scripture*. Philadelphia: Fortress, 1979.

Clifford, Richard J. "Isaiah 55: Invitation to a Feast." In *The Word of the Lord Shall Go Forth: Essays in Honor of David Noel Freedman*, edited by Carol L. Meyers and Michael O'Connor, 27–35. Winona Lake, IN: Eisenbrauns, 1983.

Delitzsch, Franz. *Biblical Commentary on the Prophecies of Isaiah*. Vol. 2. Translated by James Denny. 2 vols. New York: Funk & Wagnalls, 1890.

Eissfeldt, Otto. "The Promises of Grace to David in Isaiah 55:1–5." In *Israel's Prophetic Heritage: Essays in Honor of James Muilenburg*, edited by Bernhard W. Anderson and Walter Harrelson, 196–207. New York: Harper, 1962.

Fishbane, Michael. *Biblical Interpretation in Ancient Israel*. Oxford: Clarendon, 1985.

———. "Inner Biblical Exegesis: Types and Strategies of Interpretation in Ancient Israel." In *Midrash and Literature*, edited by Geoffrey H. Hartman and Sanford Budick, 19–37. New Haven: Yale University Press, 1986.

Gammie, John G. "On the Intention and Sources of Daniel I–VII." *VT* 31 (1981) 282–92.

———. "The Classification, Stages of Growth, and Changing Intentions in the Book of Daniel." *JBL* 95 (1976) 191–204.

Goldingay, John. "The Stories of Daniel: A Narrative Politics." *JSOT* 37 (1987) 99–116.

Hanson, Paul D. *The Dawn of Apocalyptic: The Histoical and Sociological Roots of Jewish Apocalyptic Eschatology*. Rev. ed. Philadelphia: Fortress, 1979.

———. "Israelite Religion in the Early Postexilic Period." In *Ancient Israelite Religion: Essays in Honor of Frank M. Cross*, edited by Patrick D. Miller et al., 485–508. Philadelphia: Fortress, 1987.

Hendel, Ronald S. "The Social Origins of the Aniconic Tradition in Early Israel." *CBQ* 50 (1988) 365–82.

Humphreys, W. Lee. "A Life-Style for Diaspora: A Study of the Tales of Esther and Daniel." *JBL* 92 (1973) 211–23.

Jobling, David. "Sociological and Literary Approaches to the Bible: How Shall the Twain Meet?" *JSOT* 38 (1987) 85–93.

LaCocque, André. *The Book of Daniel*. Translated by David Pellauer. 1979. Reprinted, Eugene, OR: Wipf & Stock, 2015.

Moltmann, Jürgen. *Theology and Joy*. Translated by Reinhard Ulrich. London: SCM, 1973.

Muilenburg, James. "The Book Isaiah, Chapters 40–66." In *The Interpreter's Bible*, edited by George Arthur Buttrick, 5:381–773. Nashville: Abingdon, 1956.

Murphy, Roland E. "The Kerygma of the Book of Proverbs." *Int* 20 (1966) 3–14.

Neusner, Jacob. *Midrash as Literature: The Primacy of Documentary Discourse*. 1987. Reprinted, Eugene, OR: Wipf & Stock, 2003.

———. *Understanding Seeking Faith: Essays on the Case of Judaism*. 4 vols. Brown Judaic Studies. Atlanta: Scholars, 1986.

———. *What Is Midrash?* Guides to Biblical Scholarship. Philadelphia: Fortress, 1987.

Rad, Gerhard von. *Old Testament Theology*, Vol. 2, *The Theology of Israel's Prophetic Traditions*. Translated by D. M. G. Stalker. New York: Harper & Row, 1965.

Sanders, James A. "Isaiah 55:1–9." *Int* 32 (1978) 291–95.

Schwartz, L. S., and Daniel D. Rosenberg, eds. *Congregation: Contempory Writers Read the Jewish Bible*, 420–21. San Diego: Harcourt Brace Jovanovich, 1987.

Seeligmann, I. L. "Voraussetzungen der Midraschexegese." In *Congress Volume: Copenhagen, 1953*, 150–81. VTSup 1. Leiden: Brill, 1953.

Towner, W. Sibley. *Daniel*. Interpretation. Atlanta: John Knox, 1984.

———. "Daniel 1 in the Context of the Canon." In *Canon, Theology, and Old Testament Interpretation: Essays in Honor of Brevard S. Childs*, edited by Gene M. Tucker et al., 285–98. Philadelphia: Fortress, 1988.

———. "Were the English Puritans 'The Saints of the Most High'?" *Int* 37 (1983) 46–63.

Westermann, Claus. *Isaiah 40–66: A Commentary*. Translated by David M. G. Stalker. OTL. Philadelphia: Westminster, 1969.

Wolff, Hans Walter. *Old Testament Anthropology*. Translated by Margaret Kohl. Philadelphia: Fortress, 1974.

3

Psalms 9–10:
A Counter to Conventional Social Reality

Norman Gottwald's scholarship has impinged upon our common work in crucial ways. He has placed us all in his debt, including those who do not easily follow his lead. I am pleased to register my debt through this essay. Two aspects of Gottwald's work have been in my purview for this essay. First, Gottwald has well argued that acceptance of "the final form of the text" (as in canon criticism) does not preclude a social analysis of the text, but requires it, so that we can attend to the interest and disputes that have received canonical articulation.[1] Second, Gottwald has shown that scriptural texts, like all texts, grow out of socio-economic-political reality and voice those realities, and cannot be understood apart from those realities.[2] He has been criticized (rightly in my judgment) for not treating text and social reality in a more dialectical fashion; he has, nonetheless, taught us critical lessons concerning the reality-base of a textual voice. In this essay, I will propose a rereading of Psalms 9–10 that is, in my judgment, decisively illuminated by Gottwald's scholarship.

A Conflicted Conversation

Psalms 9–10 together constitute an acrostic poem, though in the middle section the acrostic is somewhat disturbed.[3] The acrostic is nonetheless

---

1. Gottwald, "Social Matrix and Canonical Shape."

2. Jobling, "Sociological and Liteary Approaches to the Bible," has seen that Gottwald's crucial contribution is not his "peasant revolt" hypothesis, but the methodological revolution he has articulated and modeled.

3. See Gottwald's own comments on the acrostic form in *Studies in the Book of Lamentations*, 23–32. On the disorder of the acrostic sequence, see Kraus, *Psalm 1–59*,

clear enough, so that these psalms constitute a single poem (as is reflected in the LXX numbering). Though the psalm is conventionally identified as a Song of Thanksgiving, it is in fact much more complicated.[4] I will argue that these psalms together constitute the conflicted conversation that arises inevitably in an unequally organized society where the reality of Yahweh is taken into account. That conflicted conversation, however, is here presented from the perspective of the one who nowhere else is permitted any social voice.[5]

The poem of Psalms 9–10 begins as a Song of Thanksgiving that describes and celebrates a past powerful deliverance wrought by God (9:2–17). In this unit, the speaker has found an assertive voice, using a first person pronoun five times (vv. 2–3),[6] and returning to the same self-assertion twice more (v. 15).[7] The speaker's powerful voice both celebrates a new situation already in hand (vv. 2–3) and anticipates a new situation yet to be enacted by God (v. 15).

The one addressed in these verses, indeed the true subject of the song, is Yahweh. In vv. 4–7, Yahweh is directly addressed six times, each time as the subject of a powerful, active verb that describes Yahweh's action already witnessed by the speaker.[8] The actions for which Yahweh is celebrated are of two kinds. On the one hand, there are various destructive actions: "destroyed, blotted out, rooted out." On the other hand, the more powerful cluster of active verbs concerns judicial activity: "maintained my just

---

192. On consideration of some of the specific problems, see Leveen, "A Note on Psalm 10:17–18"; and Leveen, "Psalm X."

4. See the useful summary on form by Anderson, *The Book of Psalms I*, 104–6. See also Junker, "Unité, Composition et Genre Littéraire"; and Beyerlin, "Die *toda* der Heilsvergegenwärtigung." In what follows, it will be clear that questions of form are not aadequate for an understanding of the movement of the psalm. No doubt, the psalm moves from thanks to complaint. Our interpretation, however, must move beyond form to "voice" and to "interest."

5. On the capacity and power of a poem or narrative to give voice to those who have no other voice, see Engelbert, "Introduction," esp. xx. See also more generally Perry, ed., *Voices of Emergency*; and Brink, *Writing in a State of Siege*.

6. "I will give thanks, I will tell, I will be glad, I will exult, I will sing."

7. "I will recount, I will rejoice." The verb *spr* is used both in the initial statement and in the reprise.

8. "You have done [my justice], you sat, you rebuke, you destroyed, you blotted out, you rooted out." The verbal uses are "declarative" and refer to actual, concrete interventions. See Westermann, *The Praise of God in the Psalms*, 102–8 and passim; and Crüsemann, *Studien zur Formgeschichte von Hymnus und Danklied in Israel*.

cause," "gave righteous judgment," and perhaps "rebuked." It may be that even the destructive actions credited to God are done by court decree, for a verdict in court may indeed "blot out" and "root out," that is, render publicly null and void.[9] Thus the accumulation of these verbs may celebrate a day the speaker had in court, a day of total vindication.

This sense of thanksgiving is reinforced in more formal, distanced language in vv. 8-9, wherein Yahweh is described in the third person with the five terms *mišpaṭ špṭ, ṣedeq, dyn,* and *mešarim.* Thus the speaker celebrates the fact that in court, Yahweh is not only an equitable judge, but is a free agent who is not in the pocket of the wicked; God is able to take independent action, even against the presumably strong one, in behalf of the weak ones.[10] Westermann has shown that the complaint psalm characteristically involves three parties.[11] In this poem, the decisive party is Yahweh, who governs powerfully and equitably. Yahweh is the one who takes all the decisive actions. It is Yahweh, executor of judgment, whose actions determine the social position and possibility of the other two parties. The speaker's counterpart, the "enemy" (vv. 4, 7) (who is the helpless "outsider" to this textual world) is variously identified as "the nations" (vv. 6, 16, 18), the "wicked" (plural, v. 18), and the "wicked" (singular, vv. 6, 17). There seems to be no stable identity of the "enemy" in this poem, as indeed there is not generally.[12] In any case, the "enemy" is not an active, vocal party to this poem; the poem does its best, as we shall see, to commit an act of social nullification of the enemy. The poem is crafted to exclude the enemy from

---

9. Thus, for example, the petition to "blot out" in Ps 109:13-15 would seem to request judicial action. It is important for the governing metaphors of the psalm that the act of nullification need not be warlike violence, but can be the power of a severe court verdict. On the juridical metaphor in Psalm 109, see Brueggemann, "Psalm 109."

10. On the connection between justice and power, see Whitelam, *The Just King.* Characteristically, the exploited in Israel appeal to the court of Yahweh when lesser courts fail. Note that the prophets regularly inveigh against rigged courts. It is the circumstance of rigged human courts that makes appeal to the court of Yahweh a socially poignant act of rhetoric.

11. Westermann, "Struktur und Geschichte der Klage im Alten Testament." In the speech of complaint, the speaker seeks to "triangle" with God against the third party of the triangle, the enemy. On the pervasiveness of "triangling," see Bowen, *Family Therapy in Clinical Practice,* 373-76 and passim; and less directly Friedman, *Generation to Generation,* 35-39, 75-78, and passim.

12. See the review of the problem by Croft, *The Identity of the Individual in the Psalms,* 15-48. Croft is surely correct to speak of an "empty metaphor" (71) in the Psalms, so that it is not possible to trace any evolutionary development in the content of the various terms for "enemy" or for "poor."

any significant action and any determinative speech. The poem intends to render the "enemy" impotent and irrelevant.

We gain our best clue to who the "wicked" might be if we notice the identity of the third party, presumably the one who speaks in the poem, the "I" of vv. 2–3, 15. Five terms are used to describe the speaker and the ones with whom the speaker identifies and on whose behalf the poem is rendered. This is the voice of the "oppressed" (*dak*, v. 10), the "poor, afflicted" (*'anawim* or *'aniyyim*, vv. 13, 19), the "one who suffers" (*'oni*, v. 14), and the "needy" (*'ebyon*, v. 19). This cluster of words makes clear that the speaker (and those for whom the speaker speaks) are the socially vulnerable and marginal. Thus the poem is the voice of the marginated, the ones without power, resources, or authority who are vulnerable in the face of their adversaries. They have, however, found recourse in the juridical reliability of Yahweh, whose verdicts make unequal social relationships viable. It is only in this courtroom under the governance of Yahweh that the usual power relations between the strong and the weak are interrupted, transformed, and rectified, so that the weak and marginal speak here as they are permitted to speak nowhere else.

The poem is intentional and powerful in building a picture of social reality by clustering pejorative terms. On the one hand, there are "enemies, nations, wicked." On the other hand are the "oppressed, aflicted, suffering, needy, and poor." Thus the psalm deftly proposes a disputatious framing of social reality and social power. Given that framing, the poem asserts that it is only in the court of Yahweh that the second party gets a fair hearing against the first, stronger party that usually dominates court proceedings. That is a passionate theological affirmation. When one asks, however, where this peculiar court of Yahweh is convened that renders such unusual and equitable verdicts, the answer is: this odd court is convened in the poem and only in the poem. This is what makes the poem so urgent. It becomes a script and practice of counter social reality that does not seem to pertain outside the poem. This does not make the poem untrue. It only makes the poem more urgent. The thanksgiving voiced in these verses concerns precisely distorted (even if routine) social relations that have been rectified by the reality of Yahweh. The season of this alternative court extends, in the first instance, only through the lifespan of this voiced poem. When the poem ends, this odd court is adjourned.

PSALMS 9–10

Remembering and Forgetting

The guarantee of this surprisingly rectified mode of social relations depends on the resolve, attentiveness, and faithfulness of Yahweh, without whom the usual expoloitative patterns of social relations would not be broken. In v. 13, there is a pivotal juxtaposition of "remember" (*zkr*) and "forget" (*škḥ*). Everything turns on the assurance, here given vigorous affirmation, that God *remembers* and does not *forget*. The pronominal object of *zkr* is presumably Yahweh's saving deeds (*'aliliot* in v. 12, cf. *niplaʾot* in v. 2). In our context, these "saving deeds" perhaps refer to legal precedents whereby Yahweh has overturned conventional court rules that favor the strong. Yahweh remembers those precedents and knows how to continue to act in the same ways. Conversely, "forget" has as its object the cry of affliction that Yahweh has heard and continues to heed and honor. This parallelism thus affirms what is most crucial about Yahweh for this speaker:

> *saving deeds* are "remembered,"
> *cries of the afflicted* are "not forgotten."

These two are interrelated, for it is the cries of wretchedness that evoke the *deeds* of saving.[13]

The verb *zkr* is used negatively in v. 7; Yahweh has destroyed the memory of the enemy. Yahweh is clear concerning what is to be remembered. The enemy and their cities have been nullified; that is, the names are blotted out, removed from public identity and from membership in the community (v. 6). They are made to be socially irrelevant, declared by the court to be null and void. Conversely, the term "forget" is used again in v. 19 positively. The needy are not forgotten.

Verse 19 seems to be a careful, positive counterpart to the negative assertion of v. 7. Whereas the memory of the strong enemy is nullified (v. 7) the needy are not forgotten but remembered (v. 19). Both verses, v. 7 (negatively) and v. 19 (positively), use the adverb *neṣaḥ*, but to contrasting effect. The enemy is voided (*laneṣaḥ*); the poor are not forgotten (*laneṣaḥ*). Both

---

13. The structure of "cry–save" is characteristic in Israel's faith, as is reflected in the psalms of complaint, in the initiation of the Exodus narrative (Exod 2:23–25), and in songs of thanksgiving like Psalm 107. Both the cry of Israel and the deeds of Yahweh belong to the remembering of God, and it is that twofold remembering that moves God to act in the present. Boecker, *Redeformen des israelitischen Rechtslebens im Alten Testament*, 94–111, has shown that the capacity of Yahweh to remember has a juridical meaning consistent with the juridical metaphor elsewhere in the psalm. See also Childs, *Memory and Tradition in Israel*, 31–41.

verses use the verb *'bd*, one negatively and one positively. The memory of the enemy has perished (*'bd*, v. 7); the hope of the poor does not perish (*'bd*, v. 19). The uses of *zkr* (vv. 7, 13) and of *ṣkḥ* (vv. 13, 19) portray a social reversal whereby the powerful wicked have been nullified and the marginal have been given a guaranteed social position. Both received a future that is improbable in normal social transactions. The thanksgiving of vv. 2–19 celebrates a social inversion made possible because of Yahweh, but visible and concrete in the world of politics and economics, made visible by this daring poem. There is much for which to give thanks. Thus the genre of Thanksgiving Song becomes a vehicle for articulating a radically different mode of social relationship. The intent is not simply thanksgiving, but the voicing of new modes of social power.

When Yahweh is Absent

The psalm, of course, does not end at 9:19, but moves into more interesting and agitated speech. Already in vv. 14–15, the confidence of the Song of Thanksgiving has begun to erode. The verdict of Yahweh, decisive as it is, is not enduring. The power of the wicked ("the enemy," "the nations") is enormously resilient. One might have thought, and Yahweh might have intended, that the affirmation of vv. 8–9 would put an end to the destructive work of the wicked. Our own social experience, however, reminds us that the defeated, delegitimated forces of exploitation have a remarkable way of regrouping and reemerging with power and as threat.[14] It is because of that reemergence that the Song of Thanksgiving of vv. 2–19 turns to fresh and urgent appeal to Yahweh.

The petition of v. 14 is not yet very intense, and vv. 14–15 already assume a good resolution of the conflict that will culminate in praise.[15] The petition, however, becomes much more urgent in 9:20—10:2. It is as though the verdicts and assurances of 9:2–19 have not occurred, and the poor are

---

14. Thus, for example, in Nicaragua the old alliance among the Samozans reappears at the leadership of the "Contras," and in the Philippines the allies of Marcos retain control of the military. The social forces with disproportionate power find various ways in which to organize and name their exploitative power. Thus the elimination of an instrument of abuse does not eliminate the powers that propel that abuse.

15. On the anticipatory function of the song of thanksgiving, see Beyerlin, "Die *toda* der Heilsvergegenwärtigung," esp. 209–10. The purpose of such a song of thanksgiving is to foster and enact the expectation that present trouble will be resolved into well-being, as was past trouble.

again deeply at risk. Thus the voice of *thanksgiving* gives way to the voice of urgent *petition*. In 9:19 the poor have enormous hope. By 10:2, however, the same poor are in deep jeopardy, because the wicked (10:2, singular) has reappeared in the poem, and in the social reality of the speaker. This urgent petition begins with a powerful summons to God: "Arise!" The tone of the imperative suggests that the confident and reassuring verdicts of the remembered past have been discarded by the judge who made them.

The motivation to support that strong imperative is presented in a chiasm (vv. 20–21). In vv. 20–21 are two imperatives, "judge" (in *niphal*) and "put in fear." The petition asks Yahweh to do again what was earlier celebrated, to pursue and execute judgment against the exploiters. The two verbs are framed by the double use of *'enoš* with jussive verbs. That is, the ones critiqued are only human. They have therefore no right to dominate social relations. The prayer is that the threatening ones would be returned to their proper, modest social position, for they have forgotten that position and have claimed for themselves power, authority, privilege, and preeminence that never legitimately belongs to human persons.[16]

The appeal to Yahweh in 10:1 contrasts the present conduct of Yahweh with the previously celebrated conduct of Yahweh. In 9:10 Yahweh was a "stronghold in times of trouble." Now in 10:1, the same phrase is used to assert that Yahweh is absent in times of trouble; when Yahweh is absent, the wicked will devour the poor. Everything depends on Yahweh's presence, and now Yahweh is hidden. In 10:1 "stand afar off" (*beraḥoq*, which has no precise parallel in 9:9) may serve as a contrast to "not forsaken" (v. 11). That is, the God who is *afar off* has indeed forsaken the poor when they are in jeopardy. Thus both lines of 10:1 voice a strong contrast to the ranee of 9:10–11. In the contrast between 9:10–11 and 10:1, the poem closely connects *actual social relations* and the *theological reality* of God's presence or absence. The prospect for the well-being of the vulnerable in social relations depends on the initiative, attentiveness, and activity of Yahweh. Without Yahweh, the poor and afflicted are without an avenger (v. 13) and have no hope (v. 19), for "man" prevails (9:20). By 10:2, the poem has made clear

---

16. It is remarkable that Kennedy, *The Rise and Fall of the Great Powers*, analyzes recent nation-states in the same categories. His thesis is that nations overstep their rightful claim to natural resources based on territory and populations. He draws the conclusion that in the present time, the United States has overstepped its rightful share and is now having to withdraw from that overextension. Psalms 9–10 describe a situation in which the powerful have claimed excessive portions of life for themselves. On the painful and direct cost of yielding such disproportion, see Newman, *Falling from Grace*.

that everything in social relations depends on the presence or absence of Yahweh. When Yahweh is absent, social relations will take their inevitably destructive course, which the weak cannot resist. When Yahweh is present, as Yahweh may be because of urgent petition, conventional destructive relations are overcome and new social possibilities may emerge.

The Wicked Speak

In 10:3-9, the psalm takes a curious and unexpected turn. The previously identified but silent adversary is permitted to speak. A new voice speaks, one usually not heard in such a psalm, and certainly not heard heretofore in this psalm. It is the voice of the "wicked" (singular), the one who previously has been "enemy, nations, wicked" (plural).

The wicked is permitted to say and forced to say what he might prefer not to say out loud. He is required to speak what he truly intends. His actions are characteristically indirect, hiding his true intentions in ideological self-justification. Now his speech, directly quoted, goes behind the pretense to speak the unvarnished truth.[17] We are given three alleged quotes from the wicked:

> (1) "There is no God" (10:4). This statement is not presented as a direct quote, but the verbs in v. 3 ("boast," *hll*; "curse," *brk*; "renounce," *n'ṣ*) suggest self-asserting speech.[18] The wicked one acts through speech.[19]

> (2) "He thinks in his heart, 'I shall not be moved;[20] throughout all generations I shall not meet adversity'" (v. 6).

---

17. On the strategy of such quotation, see Wolff, "Das Zitat im Prophetenspruch"; and Gordis, *Poets, Prophets, and Sages*, 104-59. The inclination to quote one's adversary fits well in a juridical context in which the witness of the adversary is then refuted.

18. Leeven, "Psalm X," 17, suggests that the text be adjusted to show that the statement is indeed a direct quote. See also Gordis, *Poets, Prophets, and Sages*, 121.

19. The interplay of quoted speech and counterspeech emphasizes the social, political power of speech. As Yahweh can nullify speech, so also in human relationships, the powerful can silence the speech of the weak. Notice in the speeches of Elihu (Job 32-37) how crucial is the power of speech. On the social power of speech, see Belenky et al., *Women's Ways of Knowing*, with its accent on "listening" and "voice."

20. The term "be moved" (*mwṭ*, niphal) is characteristically used in contexts of pious obedience and devoted trust (cf. Pss 15:5; 16:8; 21:7; 30:7; 62:7; 112:6; Prov 10:30). The term is used arrogantly here to claim guaranteed well-being, but without the obedience or trust that is characteristically a condition of such assurance. Thus the quote mocks, or

(3) "He says in his heart, 'You will not call to account'" (v. 13; cf. v. 4).

All three statements are dismissals of God and assertions of self-sufficiency and autonomy. The speaker of these lines imagines he is free to do whatever he wants.

We have seen in 9:2–19 that social relations are powerfully different because Yahweh has decisively intervened as a third party. These statements attributed to the "wicked" are statements that dismiss that third party as an effective player in the drama of social interaction. The statements are insistences that social relations include only two parties, the wicked and the weak. There is no third party to intervene or to disrupt that simple, direct, and predictable transaction. The subject of these statements is "God." The intent, however, is to articulate a social reality without the inconvenient theological element of Yahweh.

We notice that all three statements are either alleged or implied. That is, they are not and do not claim to be direct, actually verbalized statements, for no one would have dared to speak so. In fact, they are not speeches or claims made by the wicked. They are rather statements attributed to the wicked but made by someone else. They are assigned and attributed speeches. Thus, in the rhetoric of this psalm, the wicked are not in fact permitted to speak for themselves but are at the mercy of those who seize the chance to speak for them. This remarkable rhetoric strategy of the psalmist places the wicked in an odd and unusual circumstance. The wicked (who are also the strong) are accustomed to speaking for themselves so that they may carefully choose what they say and what they deliberately withhold—what they want to leave unsaid. That is, their selective, self-serving speech can keep them from telling the truth about their social intentions.

Moreover, because the wicked are also the strong, the wicked are accustomed not only to speaking for themselves; they also determine when the weak are permitted to speak and what they are permitted to say. Characteristically, the wicked (= strong) control social conversations. They govern not only their own speech, but also the speech of their fragile, intimidated adversaries.

What has happened in this poem is that the wicked have lost their control of the social conversation. They no longer decide what will be uttered or who will speak; now, perhaps for the first time, the strong are at the mercy of the weak, who are free to construe conflicted social dynamics in a

---

offers a caricature of, conventional use.

very different way. Instead of the usual self-justifying, mystifying ideology of the wicked, we now get a critical expose of the actions and intentions of the wicked. Their actual intent is now placed in their own mouths as a harsh self-indictment.

The alleged statements of the wicked (in vv. 4, 6, 13) are surrounded by rhetoric that contextualizes their alleged statements, and by observed behavior that supports the adversarial construal of the speech and intent of the wicked by the weak. The supportive rhetoric is of two kinds. First, there is a series of words alluding to speech: "boast" (*hll*), "curse" (*brk*), "renounce" (*n'ṣ*) (v. 3); "puff" (*pyḥ*, v. 5); "curse" (*'lh*), "deceit" (*mirmah*), "tongue of mischief and iniquity" (v. 7). This cluster of words suggests that the wicked are so strong and influential that they can manipulate social processes, social symbols, social communication, and social decision-making in ways that further victimize the weak.[21] They have social power to arrange social relations to their own advantage.

Second, destructive speech is matched by their usurpatious actions. Thus there are these phrases, "greedy for gain" (v. 3), "sits in ambush," "murder the innocent," "watch for the hapless" (v. 8); "lurks in secret," "lurks that he may seize," "seizes the poor" (v. 9). The picture that emerges is of rapacious violence.

In this dramatic portrayal of the wicked, we have a convergence of three facts that are held together by the daring rhetoric of the poet: (1) the visible *exercise of destructive social relations in the economic realm*, (2) the *exercise of speech* as the primary way in which social power is destructively manipulated, and (3) an implicit *theological disclaimer* that removes Yahweh from the world of social reality. Violent action, manipulative speech, and nullification of God work together to permit a certam kind of social world in which the powerful are free to do what they want for their own interest. This convergence is not an occasional act of brutality, but is a systemic, ideological practice of perverse social relations. The violent acts and manipulative speech are possible only when social reality is reduced to

---

21. Mowinckel, *Psalmenstudien I*, has given the classic treatment of the "evil-doers," suggesting they are the ones who work magic. I suggest that Mowinckel's classic treatment does not sufficiently take into account the social power wielded by the the "evil-doers." It is not necessary to appeal to "magic," but simply to notice how the powerful control the social discourse of the community, that is, define the terms of social communication, and thereby manipulate social power and shape social relations to their own advantage. Those who protest against the "evil-doers" may be those who have "no voice," because the speech has all been usurped.

only unequal partners. When there are only two, the weak have no chance against the ruthless strong.

Unchallenged Power

The world as socially ordered in 10:3–9 is no doubt a polemical construal, but it is not an unknown or unrecognizable world. It is a world that everywhere exists when social relations involve only these two partners. In that brutalizing world, the wicked do not need to proceed by overt acts of ambush, lurking, and seizing. Over time, they are able to proceed by the power of their ideology.[22] When that ideology has nullified God, so that only two parties are left, it is "natural" and "obvious" that symbiosis of the power of the strong and the vulnerability of the weak is ordinary, permanent, and eventually normative. Indeed, in the reduced world it is the only imagmable mode of social relations; that is, the power of the strong controls the weak. The ideology of the strong assaults the weak until the victims of wrong social relations accept the world as defined by the perpetrators.[23] Thus unchallenged power is eventually accepted as legitimate.

That mode of social relations prevails almost everywhere—except in this psalm and in like assertions of counter-reality. In such assertions, the ideology of the wicked is given full, albeit hostile, voicing in order that the ideology of the strong may be exposed, critiqued, and overthrown. Thus I propose that 10:3–9, when taken alone, are a fairly standard script, albeit kept invisible and unvoiced for uncritical social relations. This psalm is an extraordinary act of counterspeech and counterpower. It seizes the conventional, usually unquestioned, script of the strong, states it, mocks it, and overrides it, so that the psalm itself is a moment of social inversion

---

22. Lenski, *Power and Privilege*, an important influence on Gottwald, has shown how raw material power inevitably depends on the power of ideology, and not sheer force, for the establishment and maintenance of legitimate poetic portrayal. On the control of social *ideology* by the powerful in the interest of their *property*, see Meeks, *God the Economist*, 202 and passim. Note the use he makes of the work of Froman, *The Two American Polical Systems*.

23. On the crucial power to define, see Morrison, *Beloved*, 190. "Clever, but school teacher beat him anyway to show him that definitions belonged to the definers—not the defined." More programmatically, Karl Marx concluded, "The ruling ideas of each age have ever been the ideas of its ruling class" (McLellan, *The Thought of Karl Marx*, 46). Gaventa, *Power and Powerlessness,* has reviewed a dramatic case in which control of the categories of communication and perception forecloses all social possibilities.

and even social control for those who normally are left without speech and without power.

There can hardly be any doubt whose voice sounds in this psalm. It is the voice of the oppressed, the afflicted, the suffering, the needy, the poor, who are endlessly pursued until they cease to exist. Although usually denied voice, they nonetheless speak boldly in this psalm. They have finally, through this poem, gained the floor, and they speak without interruption. Indeed, they will not let anyone else speak, for they know that if the wicked begin to speak, their ideology will again usurp social relations. The marginal have spoken first in celebration of the "third party" (Yahweh) who changes social relations (9:2–19). Then they have issued a plea for the continued presence of that third party (9:20—10:3). Then they have mockingly reiterated the speech of the powerful, who reduce social relations to two parties and by their speech eliminate the dangerous third party (10:3–9).

After their mocking attribution of speech to the strong, the weak ones now return to their own situation and their own social insistence (10:10–18). In vv. 10–11, the voice of the poor candidly reports their intimidated response to the ideological onslaught of the wicked. The marginal had almost succumbed to the assertions and definitions of the wicked. That is, they had well-nigh accepted the portrayal of social reality offered by the wicked in 10:3–9 (cf. Ps 73:10–14). The poor had nearly yielded to the self-serving ideology of the wicked. The poor experienced a failure of nerve, and the courageous rhetoric of 9:2–19 was almost abandoned. The poor are crushed and fallen, that is, ready to submit without a struggle. We have seen the arrogant wicked who "thinks in his heart," who has evil purposes he wants kept hidden. In 10:11, we now are permitted access to the hidden thinking of the vulnerable. The dispute between the wicked and the poor concerns the reality of God. What is "hidden" has to do with the autonomy of the powerful and the despair of the poor. The latter think:

> God has forgotten,
> God has hidden his face,
> God will never see it. (v. 11)

The first phrase echoes 9:19, only now that vigorous, confident assertion has become a despairing resignation. What was vigorously affirmed in 9:19 is now reluctantly abandoned. The wicked have won the battle for the imagination, and the thoughts of the poor have come to mirror and replicate

PSALMS 9-10

the thoughts of the wicked.[24] The wicked have imagined God away, and the poor now accept that verdict. The world without God (who is hidden, 10:11; cf. v. 1) is a hopeless world for the poor. The poor accept the ideology of the powerful.

In 10:12, however, the psalm takes a most unexpected turn. The psalm might have ended in v. 11 in defeat and resignation. Verse 12, however, is discontinuous from the forlornness of v. 11. The powerful petition of vv. 12-13 must have been a surprise to the wicked, who had counted on the resignation of their victims in vv. 10-11. It must equally have been a surprise to the poor, who, in the same verses, had indeed lost hope. Indeed, the imperative of v. 12 is an inexplicable non sequitur after vv. 10-11.

That, however, is exactly the work of the psalm as a political act. It is the psalm as a voice of inexplicable hope, surely rooted in an unquenchable sense of Yahweh as a third party in social relations, that in its utterance creates a new social possibility that did not exist before or outside this utterance. It is the political work of the poet, by an act of daring rhetoric, to create a new social possibility by negating the dominant ideology of 10:3-9 and by countering it with a liberated imperative.[25]

The imperative of 10:12 begins at the same place as did the imperative of 9:20: "Arise!" In 9:20, however, the imperative follows a statement of hope, a conviction of not being forgotten (9:19). Now, however, the same imperative follows an admission of hopelessness and a sense of being forgotten by God (10:10-11). The imperative of v. 12 is inexplicable, except as an act of political counterimagination rooted in theological passion.[26] Any other explanation of the unexpected imperative is perforce ruled out, because any other explanation seeks to accommodate the dominate ideol-

---

24. On the battle for imagination, see Wilder, *Jesus' Parables and the War of Myths.*

25. On the power and responsibility of fictive words, story, and poem, see Engelbert, "Introduction," xiii-ixx. She writes:
> Occasionally this amputation of history, coupled with a rigid censorship, was successful in colonizing the imagination . . . Against the powerful ideologies imposing themselves in the isthmus, the ancient strategies of the embattled storyteller—parable and allegory, parody and saire, fable and fantastic tale—were in colonial times, as now, invaluable arms in the struggle to ransom the abducted past, to delineate and to denounce a repressive present.

26. See the works of Engelbert, Perry, and Brink, cited in notes 5 and 25 above. For a more programmatic treatment of the power of imagination to create an alternative, see Green, *Imagining God.* Green does not pursue the subversive element of imagination, but his stress on "as" as the "copulative of imagination" suggests that subversive poetry and narrative see the world differently, and not "as" the dominant culture proposes.

ogy that the strong must prevail and that Yahweh is no social agent. Imaginative, liberated rhetoric precludes conventional explanations, primarily because this rhetoric arises outside the field of acceptable explanation and posits a genuine novum, new politically, rhetorically, and theologically.

The name of Yahweh is regularly on the lips of the speaker (9:2, 8, 10, 11, 12, 14, 20, 21; 10:1). That name has been absent in the speech of the wicked (10:3–9), who want to eliminate Yahweh politically and rhetorically.[27] The alleged rhetoric of the wicked speaks only of "God," who is easier to eliminate than is "Yahweh."[28] Now in 10:12, the name of Yahweh is again invoked as an active, decisive agent. In the remainder of the psalm, God is addressed directly, whereas the wicked speak of God only as a remote third party who is assumed not to be present to the conversation. In vv. 14–18, the address is completely to Yahweh. The rhetoric is saturated with "thou" (as in vv. 5–7); Yahweh is again a real agent who controls decisive verbs. The verbal form is matched by pronominal suffixes that place Yahweh at the center of the poem.

This passionate rhetoric waits on Yahweh to intrude decisively into skewed social relations, to act decisively against the wicked, who imagine they are autonomous. The object of God's concern is the afflicted (v. 12), the fatherless (v. 14), the meek (v. 17), the fatherless and oppressed (v. 18); that is, the socially marginal, powerless, and vulnerable. The hope of this voice is for justice. Appeal is made through a majestic political metaphor of enthronement, which echoes 9:8 (v. 16).

The text is a script for an alternative construal of social relations. In this script, Yahweh is an active agent. Moreover, by the end of the psalm, the wicked have been eliminated as an active force and are only the object of God's terrible intention (10:15). The intrusion of Yahweh into social relationships decisively transforms the prospect of both the wicked and the poor.

---

27. To be sure, Yahweh is mentioned in 10:3, but only with the verb *n'ṣ*, that is, only in order to be mocked. There is no genuine acknowledgment of Yahweh in the alleged quote of the wicked.

28. It is worth noting that in the poem of Job, which deals with issues very much like our psalms, the entire discussion of Job and his friends never mentions Yahweh, but only "God." It is only in 38:1 that Yahweh now speaks. It is the intrusion and voice of this specific God that shatters the argument. Whereas the earlier discussion tended to eliminate Yahweh, in fact it is the voice of Yahweh that nullifies the earlier discussion. On the attempt to eliminate Yahweh (as the wicked have done in Psalm 10), see Tsevat, *The Meaning of the Book of Job*, 35–37. See also Neher, *The Exile of the Word*, 27–30.

This text is itself a practice of alternative politics. It is not mere wishful thinking, nor is it a description of what happened elsewhere. The psalm itself. each time it is boldly uttered in its criticism, polemic, celebration, and anticipation, is the place of redefined power relations.[29] In the rhetoric of this psalm, it is impossible to sort out what is theological (for Yahweh is a function of counter-politics) and what is political (for social conflict is a function of Yahweh's purpose and presence).[30] Everything depends on the psalm as an act of political imagination. Without the psalm, Yahweh would never be present, and social relations would forever be the two-party transaction envisioned by the ideology of the wicked. The psalm creates a possibility for energy, courage, hope, and imagination that orders political power differently.

Conclusion

This reading of Psalms 9-10 suggests that the (repeated) utterance of the poem is indeed a political act. The psalm asserts a shaping of the social process that contradicts the conventional ideology of the powerful. Although the psalms may indeed make a theological point—namely, that there is a God to whom to appeal against the nullification of that God by the ideology of the powerful—the practical, and I believe intended, effect of the psalms is to create a zone of social possibility outside the ideology of the powerful.

In this reading, we may reflect on three issues that derive from Gottwald's work. First, reading the "final form of the text" does not preclude but requires social-scientific criticism in order to hear the text. What is canonized is not a settled consensus of theological affirmation, but a conflictual conversation in which the wicked and the poor hold contrary views of the reality and pertinence of God. It is the ongoing conflict that is canonized. Moreover, in canonical form, what is normative is that both

---

29. Morrison, *Beloved*, is a clear example of the way in which fictive writing can effect the redefinition of power relationships. Clearly, the novel functions so that as the central character herself arrives at a self, the implied reader at the same time is moved toward a liberated self. In the narrative, the "defined" seizes the power of definition (cf. n. 23 above).

30. On the dialectic of "function" see Gottwald, *The Tribes of Yahweh*, 608-21. The characterization of Yahwism as "the function of socio-political equality" has obviously caused much trouble for Gottwald. The matter needs to be carfully nuanced, but Gottwald's argument is in any case important, more important than his facile critics allow.

sides of the social-theological dispute are rendered through the polemical, critical voice of the poor. In this reading of social reality, the poor not only (finally) have their say, but they also are permitted to construe the say of the wicked. This final form no doubt counters other "forms" of rendering social reality in which the decisive say is said by the powerful. The final form of the text thus protests against and offers an alternative to conventional social renderings. The convergence of "final form" and "countersay" is unavoidable in reading this text critically.

Second, the religious claim of the text arises from concrete socio-economic-political reality. One could hardly imagine this text being framed without direct and intimate connection to social reality. Indeed, any reading of the poem, such as genre analysis, that ignores this interface to social reality will likely miss hearing the psalm.[31] The God-question is situated exactly in a social dispute between the wicked who say "There is no God" and the poor who say "God has forgotten," and yet who voice an urgent imperative to that same God who has forgotten. The dispute about God is clearly not an innocuous religious question, but a life-and-death dispute about the nature of social reality, social power, and social possibility.

Third, however, Gottwald's characteristic premise that the text arises from social reality is, in my judgment, not sufficiently dialectical.[32] If the text only arises from social experience, I imagine that the text might have ended in 10:11, when the poor accept the claims of the wicked. Psalm 10:12, however, breaks beyond such social experience and voices a genuine *novum* that is the work of the text. Thus I suggest that not only does the text receive its voice of advocacy from social reality, but it also speaks its countervoice back against social reality in a way that contradicts accepted social reality and therefore social power. This latter maneuver makes clear that the text cannot be explained solely from social reality. There is no doubt that the text is a function of social experience. Gottwald allows, but does not greatly appreciate, that the text also leads reality, so that reality is a function of the

---

31. See Buss, "The Study of Forms." It has been especially Gerstenberger who has paid attention to the sociology of the psalms.

32. See Gottwald, *The Tribes of Yahweh*, 883–916; and Gottwald, "The Theological Task." Gottwald has clearly moved on theologically in the meantime. No doubt the debate will continue concerning whether such a dialectical notion of "function" is a workable articulation for theology. My own impression is that our theological work operates in this way, either above the table or beneath it. We have no choice but to let our theology function in relation to socioeconomic reality and power. To deny this linkage is to engage in self-deception. It is to imagine that when we interpret we can preclude "advocacy."

text. How or why the text is capable of this free, unfettered say is beyond our work here. That question leads through the affirmation that the text is a political act, to questions of revelation and imagination.

This rereading is informed, as best I understand it, by questions Gottwald has taught us. In appraising his work, we may ask whether Gottwald's questions matter and whether we read differently because of his work. They do, and we do! As a result, the conventional ideology does not have a final say in this text, nor in our reading of it.

Bibliography

Anderson, A. A. *The Book of Psalms I*. New Century Bible. Greenwood, SC: Attic, 1972.
Belenky, Mary Field et al. *Women's Ways of Knowing: The Development of Self, Voice, and Mind*. New York: Basic Books, 1986.
Beyerlin, Walter. "Die *toda* der Heilsvergegenwärtigung in den Klageliedern des Einzelnen." *ZAW* 79 (1967) 208–24.
Boecker, Hans Jochen. *Redeformen des israelitischen Rechtslebens im Alten Testament*. WMANT 14. Neukirchen-Vluyn: Neukirchener, 1964.
Bowen, Murray. *Family Therapy in Clinical Practice*. New York: Aronson, 1978.
Brueggemann, Walter. "Psalm 109: Three Times 'Steadfast Love.'" *Word & World* 5 (1985) 144–54.
Buss, Martin J. "The Study of Forms." In *Old Testament Form Criticism*, edited by John H. Hayes, 31–56. San Antonio: Trinity University Press, 1974.
Childs, Brevard S. *Memory and Tradition in Israel*. SBT 1/37. Chicago: Allenson, 1962.
Croft, Steven J. L. *The Identity of the Individual in the Psalms*. JSOTSup 44. Sheffield: Sheffield Academic, 1987.
Crüsemann, Frank. *Studien zur Formgeschichte von Hymnus und Danklied in Israel*. WMANT 32. Neukirchen-Vluyn: Neukirchener, 1969.
Engelbert, Jo Ann. "Introduction." In *And We Sold the Rain: Contemporary Fiction from Central America*, edited by Rosario Santos, ix–xxiii. New York: Four Walls Eight Windows, 1988.
Friedman, Edwin. *Generation to Generation: Family Process in Church and Synagogue*. Guilford Family Therapy Series. New York: Guilford, 1985.
Froman, Creel. *The Two American Political Systems: Society, Economics, and Politics*. Englewood Cliffs, NJ: Prentice-Hall, 1984.
Gaventa, John. *Power and Powerlessness: Quiescence and Rebellion in an Appalachian Valley*. Urbana: University of Illinois Press, 1980.
Gordis, Robert. *Poets, Prophets, and Sages*. Bloomington: Indiana University Press, 1971.
Gottwald, Norman K. "Social Matrix and Canonical Shape." *ThTo* 42 (1985) 307–21. Reprinted in Norman K. Gottwald, *The Hebrew Bible in Its Social World and in Ours*, 177–92. Semeia Studies. Atlanta: Scholars, 1993.
———. *Studies in the Book of Lamentations*. SBT 1/14. Chicago: Allenson, 1954.
———. "The Theological Task after *The Tribes of Yahweh*." In *The Bible and Liberation: Political and Social Hermeneutics*, edited by Norman K. Gottwald and Richard Horsley, 190–200. Maryknoll, NY: Orbis, 1983.

———. *The Tribes of Yahweh: A Sociology of the Religion of Liberated Israel, 1250–1050 B.C.E.* Maryknoll, NY: Orbis, 1979.
Green, Garrett. *Imagining God: Theology and the Religious Imagination.* San Francisco: Harper & Row, 1989.
Jobling, David. "Sociological and Literary Approaches to the Bible: How Shall the Twain Meet?" *JSOT* 38 (1987) 85–93.
Junker, H. "Unité, Composition et Genre Littéraire des Psaumes IX et X." *Revue biblique* 60 (1953) 161–69.
Kennedy, Paul. *The Rise and Fall of the Great Powers: Economic Change and Military Conflict From 1500 to 2000.* New York: Random House, 1987.
Kraus, Hans-Joachim. *Psalms 1–59: A Commentary.* Translated by Hilton C. Oswald. Continental Commentaries. Minneapolis: Augsburg, 1988.
Lenski, Gerhard. *Power and Privilege: A Theory of Social Stratification.* 2nd ed. Chapel Hill: University of North Carolina Press, 1984.
Leveen, J. "A Note on Psalm 10:17–18." *JBL* 67 (1948) 149–50.
———. "Psalm X: A Reconstruction." *JTS* 45 (1944) 16–21.
McLellan, D. *The Thought of Karl Marx.* London: Macmillan, 1971.
Meeks, M. Douglas. *God the Economist: The Doctrine of God and Political Economy.* Minneapolis: Fortress, 1989.
Morrison, Toni. *Beloved.* New York: Knopf, 1987.
Mowinckel, Sigmund. *Psalmenstudien I: Awan und die individuellen Klagepsalmen.* 1922. Reprinted, Amsterdam: Schippers, 1961.
Neher, André. *The Exile of the Word: From the Silence of the Bible to the Silence of Auschwitz.* Translated by David Maisel. Philadelphia: Jewish Publication Society, 1981.
Newman, Katherine S. *Falling from Grace: The Experience of Downward Mobility in the American Middle Class.* Glencoe, IL: Free Press, 1988.
Tsevat, Mattiyahu. *The Meaning of the Book of Job and Other Biblical Studies.* New York: Ktav, 1980.
Westermann, Claus. *The Praise of God in the Psalms.* Translated by Keith R. Crim. Richmond: John Knox, 1965.
———. "Structure and History of Lament in the Old Testament." In *Praise and Lament in the Psalms,* 165–213. Translated by Keith R. Crim and Richard N. Soulen. Atlanta: John Knox, 1981.
———. "Struktur und Geschichte der Klage im Alten Testament." In *Forschung am Alten Testament,* 269–95. ThBü 24. Munich: Kaiser, 1964.
Whitelam, Keith W. *The Just King: Monarchical Judicial Authority in Ancient Israel.* JSOTSup 12. Sheffield: JSOT Press, 1979.
Wilder, Amos N. *Jesus' Parables and the War of Myths: Essays on Imagination in the Scripture.* Philadelphia: Fortress, 1982.
Wolff, Hans Walter. "Das Zitat im Prophetenspruch." In *Gesammelte Studien zum Alten Testament,* 36–129. ThBü 22. Munich: Kaiser, 1964.

4

Prophetic Imagination toward Social Flourishing

"Part of the ideology of the market," Tim Gorringe has written, "is that there is no alternative, but this is false. There are realistic alternatives."[1] To see that "another world is possible,"[2] however, requires an act of imagination: emancipatory imagination.

Surplus Value

The procurement of "surplus value" requires a sustained strategy for accumulation and adequate institutions for sustaining that strategy. In a state economy that strategy is through law that continually transfers wealth from labor to capital or, in Old Testament categories, from "peasants" to "urban elites." In a corporate economy the strategy is the vigorous enactment of market ideology that squeezes production schedules and arranges the social infrastructure for the sake of maximum profits. In the Western world, most particularly in the United States, that strategy is a combination of state and corporate economy in which the government is tilted, if not controlled, by lobbyists who act in the interest of corporate power by ensuring a minimum of public regulation. The outcome either way—state economy, corporate economy, or a combination of the two—is a sustained and effective process of accumulation of surplus value, not without high social cost.

The course of surplus value requires, in addition to a friendly government, centralized institutions that are unembarrassed about the ends

1. Gorringe, *Capital and the Kingdom*, 164.
2. Gorringe, *Harvest*, 133.

of privilege that they serve. On the one hand, such accumulation requires an effective military establishment, because surplus value inevitably levies a high cost from some in society who may eventually act forcefully against centralized privilege. On the other hand, such social entitlement requires a central bank for protection, investment, and growth of surplus value for the stakeholders who constitute a small minority of the population.

Solomon as Accumulator

In the world of ancient Israel, the strategy for accumulation and maintenance of surplus value was enacted and epitomized by King Solomon, who is the quintessential accumulator.[3] Indeed, one need only read of the extravagance of the royal apparatus (1 Kgs 4:22-28), the monopoly of learning (4:29-34), the extravagance of his building projects (7:1-12), the ostentatious display of gold in his new temple (6:20-22; 7:48-51), and the gain of his international commerce (10:14-25) in order to see that he was a most successful accumulator, ending with material accumulation matched by his accumulation of women, no doubt in the interest of a network of powerful alliances (11:3). This narrative report of accumulation is so over the top as to suggest that it may be offered as a mocking caricature of the ways of surplus wealth.

Almost in passing it is reported that Solomon had a standing army, no doubt for purposes of exhibit and intimidation: "So Solomon rebuilt Gezer, Lower Beth-horon, Baalath, Tamar in the wilderness, within the land, as well as all of Solomon's storage cities, the cities for his chariots, the cities for his cavalry, and whatever Solomon desired to build in Jerusalem, in Lebanon, and in all the land of his dominion ... Solomon gathered together chariots and horses; he had fourteen hundred chariots and twelve thousand horses, which stationed in the chariot cities and with the king in Jerusalem" (1 Kgs 9:17-19; 10:26). His military capacity, moreover, was reinforced by his success as an arms dealer who apparently controlled the flow of armaments in the international arena due to his strategic geographical location (1 Kgs 10:28).

The matter of a central bank is not obvious for Solomon. But the detailed description of his tax-collecting apparatus suggests the constant flow of internal revenue to the central government (4:7-19) that was matched by the immense flow of international tribute (10:23-25). We are not told where

---

3. See Brueggemann, *Solomon*.

all of that revenue was kept and invested or from where it was dispensed; but we do know that the temple functioned as such a financial center in that ancient world. Thus we may "doubleread" the narrative about the temple (1 Kgs 5–8) that was designed to be not only a "royal chapel" but also as an ostentatious gathering point for unimaginable wealth. If we equate temple with bank, we may better understand why the temple became a target of protest and judgment.[4] Thus Solomon has all the necessary equipment to procure and maintain surplus value.

The matter is not different in the economy of the United States that operates with a central bank and central bankers who are practitioners of outrageous wealth. The recent "stimulus package" gives ample evidence of how the government is in collusion with the managers of surplus wealth, a collusion that did not evoke protest until the Republican Party—by any read, the party of big wealth—caught on to the potential of populist resentment.

Clearly, the military establishment of the current lone superpower indicates that a broad military strategy is required to maintain economic advantage in the pursuit of natural resources and in the development of amenable markets.[5] Chalmers Johnson has well chronicled the way in which US militarism is now world-defining and, given market ideology, has its way in public imagination with almost no protest.[6]

Alongside military capacity and a central bank, a third prerequisite for surplus value is cheap labor or, as given in the Solomonic narrative, "forced labor": those not able to receive or enjoy the full fruit of labor. In ancient Israel, forced labor is identified as an important component of Solomon's economy (5:13–18; 9:20–23), a component that undoubtedly reflects the exodus narrative in which more-ancient Hebrews are remembered as building store cities for Pharaoh's surplus wealth (see Gen 47:13–26; Exod 1:11–14; 5:4–21). On the storage cities, see 1 Kgs 9:19, surely an allusion back to that chilling exodus memory. In the US market economy we of course do not practice or speak of "forced labor"—except that what passes for health care policy keeps working people fearfully attached to their jobs, lest they "lose coverage."

---

4. The most direct and telling critique of the temple is in Jer 7:1–15 where the temple is attacked and a bid is made for justice for widows and orphans. The two accounts are intimately connected to each other.

5. The claim of the United States as the only and final superpower is a quite provisional claim; see Jacques, *When China Rules the World*.

6. Johnson, *Blowback*; Johnson, *Nemesis*; Johnson, *Sorrows of Empire*.

What strikes one about this complex power arrangement—ancient or contemporary—is that it is a totalizing system that intends to contain all possible social options, that allows for no deviation from ideological orthodoxy concerning "God and Country." That power arrangement, moreover, precludes any initiative outside this totality. It is, for some, a soft velvet totalitarian system that makes promises to all but keeps promises only to some.

Passion and Commitment to the Common Good

When we come to Tim Gorringe's category of "flourishing," it is clear that such an exploitative system that coercively transfers wealth from the weak to the strong cannot, in the long run, "flourish." Social flourishing depends upon passion for and commitment to the common good. It is axiomatic that coercive exploitation—whether by the state, corporation, or market economy—cannot create an environment for such flourishing. That much is clear upon any serious reflection, for such exploitation produces social hostility and a refusal, if not an inability, to act humanely toward the common good. And if our reflection is not to be trusted, then the facts on the ground lead to the same conclusion. It is clear in the United States that we are at a near stalemate between centralized interests and what people perceive as the common good. If we take "safety and happiness" as shorthand measures of the common good, then it is clear that a combination of state–corporate interests have not made us safe. Indeed, such aggressive militarism contributes to a lack of safety, both because of the production of external enemies and the generation of internal hostility. Nor has that combination made us happy by any social index. It was, of course, not different in the regime of Solomon that ended with: (a) a dire judgment against the regime voiced in theological terms (2 Kgs 11:1–12); (b) a series of rebellions (11:14–22, 23–25, 26–40); (c) a prophetically instigated coup (11:31–39); and (d) eventually, a tax revolt that divided the state (12:1–24). Many opponents of Solomon—religious, political, and economic—clearly saw that such a power arrangement would never generate "flourishing."

Cry and Response

If the totalizing purview of military capitalism—a combination of state and corporate interests propelled by an ideology of acquisitiveness—cannot keep its promises, then it is required to think "outside the box" of such totalizing claims. It is by no means clear that such thinking is possible (leave alone permitted), and Slavoj Žižek judges that such thought in our contemporary context is not possible.[7] It may well be that our circumstance of totalism is unprecedented and for the first time such thought is impossible. More likely, every such context, ancient and modern, has led to the same judgment about the practical impossibility of an alternative to the "facts on the ground" or better, to the ideology that voices those "facts on the ground."

It is for that reason that such thoughts turn, finally, perhaps inevitably, to the Hebrew Bible and to the odd, inexplicable "voice" that speaks in that enigmatic, unsettled, unsettling tradition. All the way back to the exodus narrative, this tradition imagines and stages a dialogical transaction that constitutes a subversion of the monologue of military acquisitiveness. In the exodus narrative the dialogic transaction that produces daring revolutionary energy is an exchange between *the cry of the oppressed* and *the responses of Holy Resolve* that dwells outside the totalizing system of Pharaoh: "After a long time the king of Egypt died. The Israelites groaned under their slavery, and cried out. Out of the slavery their cry for help rose up to God. God heard the groaning, and God remembered his covenant with Abraham, Isaac, and Jacob. God looked upon the Israelites, and God took notice of them" (Exod 2:23–25). The cry, the voice of the oppressed, broke the silence of totalism; the slaves went public with their pain that was imposed by the exploitative system and thereby honored and owned their suffering. This act of speaking pain had to wait until a propitious moment when "the king of Egypt died." When that moment came, it is impossible to over-appreciate the transforming energy set in motion by that daring, subversive act of bringing imposed pain to public speech.

And of course, the response of Holy Resolve is equally stunning. The slaves who cried out did not address anyone; they only "groaned under their slavery and cried out." Unbeknownst to them, there was a Listener who attended to the cry and who answered in a resolve to transform (see

---

7. Žižek, *Universal Exception*, 159: "It is practically impossible effectively to call into question the logic of Capital: even a modest social-democratic attempt to redistribute wealth beyond the limit acceptable to Capital 'effectively' leads to an economic crisis, inflation, a fall in revenues and so on. Nevertheless, one should always bear in mind the way that the connection between 'cause' (rising social expenditure) and 'effect' (economic crisis) is not a direct, objective causal one; it is always-already embedded in a situation of social antagonism and struggle."

also Exod 3:7–10). That exchange, before which Pharaoh is helpless, set in motion a revolutionary history that created an opening for covenantal politics and covenantal economics wholly precluded by Pharaoh.[8]

The same dynamic is assumed and enacted in Psalm 10,[9] which, like the exodus narrative, relentlessly insists that there are three rather than two actors in the human drama. There are *the exploiters* who say:

> God will not seek it out . . .
> There is no God . . .
> We shall not be moved;
> Throughout all the generations we shall not meet adversity . . .
> God has forgotten,
> He has hidden his face, he will never see it . . .
> You will not call us to account.
> (Ps 10:4, 6, 11, 13)[10]

There are *the exploited* who here speak as they cannot elsewhere in the public domain. Most surprisingly, they cannot only describe the unbearable situation in which they find themselves, they can also muster the courage to speak an imperative that is not elsewhere permitted them. The imperative is not addressed to the exploiters from whom they expect nothing. It is addressed, rather, to the same Holy Resolve that answered back in the narrative. That is, subsequent dialogic discourse replicates that ancient memory, only now the groan and cry know whom to address:

> Rise up, O Yahweh; O God, lift up your hand;
> do not forget the oppressed . . .
> But you do see! Indeed, you note trouble and grief,
> that you may take it into your hands;
> the helpless commit themselves to you;
> you have been the helper of the orphan.
> Break the arm of the wicked and evildoers;
> seek out their wickedness until you find none.
> (vv. 12, 14, 15)

---

8. See Walzer, *Exodus and Revolution*.

9. On this psalm, see Brueggemann, "Psalm 9–10."

10. To be sure, the "exploiters" are presented through the lens of the exploited; there is no suggestion that this is "objective" characterization.

The speech culminates in (a) a doxology that assigns legitimate power to Yahweh and away from Pharonic agents (v. 16) and (b) a confident expectation for justice (vv. 17–18):

> Yahweh is king forever and ever;
> > the nations shall perish from his land.
> O Yahweh, you will hear the desire of the meek;
> > you will strengthen their heart, you will incline your ear
> to do justice for the orphan and the oppressed,
> > so that those from earth may strike terror no more.
> (vv. 16, 17–18)

The third party, *Yahweh*, does not speak here. In the tradition, however, there is divine answer. It is the reality of divine answer, all the way back to Exod 2:24–25, that is the ground for continued trust in Yahweh beyond the power of the system. Clearly this psalm is uttered on the assumption of such a responsive holiness.

The characteristic divine answer, so well described by Patrick Miller, is a salvation oracle, wherein God speaks, acknowledges the cry for help, and promises active, transformative engagement:

> There are many indications that the prayers are heard and answered. Sometimes this is a matter of direct testimony, particularly in the psalm prayers where there is no context to discover the outcome of the prayer except as it is conveyed within the prayer itself or in the song of thanksgiving that follows the prayer. Indeed it is in such testimony that the close connection of the song of thanksgiving to the prayer for help is indicated. One such song, Psalm 34, provides a kind of paradigm of the structure of prayer in Scripture and enables us to see the movement that is initiated in the relationship between God and the person in need when a cry for help goes up, when prayer is uttered:

> > I sought Yahweh, and he answered me,
> > > and delivered me from all my fears.
> > Look to him, and be radiant;
> > > so your faces shall never be ashamed.
> > This poor soul [i.e., afflicted] cried,
> > > and was heard by Yahweh,
> > > and was saved from every trouble. (vv. 4–6)

"The one who prayed is identified as an 'afflicted' person. The term may have to do with humility and meekness, but, in the context of the prayer for help, it is also to be understood as an indication of the distress of the suppliant—literally poor and weak, afflicted or oppressed."[11]

The clearest example, cited by Miller, is found in the poetry of Lamentations that seeks divine help after the destruction of Jerusalem.

> I called on your name, O Yahweh,
>   from the depths of the pit;
> you heard my plea . . .
> You came near when I called on you;
>   you said, "Do not fear!" (Lam 3:55–57)

The "do not fear" of the divine answerer is an act that intends to override the awesome, intimidating, threatening power of monological coercion. It is to be noticed that in the first instance, such divine resolve does not "do" anything, but only aims to dissolve fear. Surely the intent is that the "fearless" will not cede reality over to the ideological claims of the acquisitive engine of oppression.

Exposing the Imagination of the Regime

Our focus in what follows is upon the divine resolve that is evoked by the subversive public voicing of pain. Scholars suggest that this stylized answer is given by a designated human agent, a priest or an elder. That human agency opens, of course, the question of what traction such a theological-liturgical claim has in the midst of Realpolitik, and whether it is necessary to be a "believer" in order to enact such dramatic force. No doubt those who generated and trusted such a textual tradition and practice "believed" in the reality of such a dialogic transaction. But even short of that, one can see that what is performed is an instance of "guerilla theatre" whereby the dominant claims of coercive power are exposed as inadequate and less than compelling.[12] Clearly, performing "outside the box" is a characteristic strategy against monological power for which we have many twentieth-century examples. Such "theological performance" serves to deabsolutize the claims of the regime. Thus, in Exodus 2, Pharaoh is exposed as penultimate by

---

11. Miller, *They Cried to the Lord*, 136.
12. I take the phrase from Wilder, *Theopoetic*, 28.

the cries of the slaves and the divine response. In the prophetic oracle of 1 Kgs 11:31–39, Solomon and his claim are placed in deep jeopardy. And in Psalm 10, the poetry imagines a "resurrection" ("Rise up") of power from outside the zone of the wicked exploiters.

In all three cases the textual utterance, no doubt performed in some public venue (Passover?), attests to a reality (or a reality in waiting in Psalm 10) that is beyond the control or intimidation of the acquisitive enterprise. All three cases of narrative, oracle, and psalm constitute acts of imagination that expose the imagination of the regime as faulty, inadequate, and eventually false.[13] Regime imagination is displaced and overridden (in the performance) by an act of imagination that digs deeper into a claim for holiness. For after all, a regime that traffics in exploitation can only make a very thin claim for grounding in God's holiness. Whether and to what extent the alternative performance is persuasive remains open in each new usage, for to be persuaded by the alternative imagination is to embrace an immediate and concrete risk; but the tradition attests that it does happen.

Promises in the Face of Protest

I focus now on the divine response (to the cry) that is voiced in prophetic oracle. It is my thesis that prophetic oracles of promise imagine a social reality in which there can be social flourishing; put negatively, where there is no such promissory imagination, social flourishing is all but impossible. A sub-note to this claim is the fact that we have all too often thought of "prophetic ministry" as critique, as an act of righteous indignation against established power. There is, to be sure, such a component to the prophets in ancient Israel. Here, however, I focus on a neglected theme in prophetic utterance: promises that are indeed responses to situations of unbearable dismay that are voiced as protest and petition.

Micah 4:1–5

This text, well known on its own, is placed in the book of Micah as a response to the harsh oracle of 3:9–12 that anticipates the destruction of Jerusalem, due precisely to the acquisitive exploitation of that city and its leadership.

---

13. On out-imagining the imagination of the regime, see Cavanaugh, *Torture and Eucharist*, 278–81 and passim.

We may, for our purposes, imagine a pause between 3:12 and 4:1, a pause that allows for the implementation of the threat of 3:9–12, namely, the destruction of the city, which in turn evokes the lament of those who witness the demise of the city. Of itself the move from 3:12 to 4:1 is abrupt and makes little sense. But if we "fill in" the space between the two, we may see that the promise of 4:1–5 is a divine response to a lament over the failed city, the same dramatic sequence that we see in the book of Lamentations.

While Micah's listeners may imagine a city still engaged in injustice (3:9–11) or a city now in ruins (v. 12), this new oracle in 4:1–5 imagines out beyond both acquisitiveness and destruction. The new imagination of a newly organized city is given in a human oracle that purports to be divine intentionality (see Isa 2:1). That is, in the promise of God, the potential of Jerusalem is not confined to the scope of dominant imagination nor is it defined by destruction, anticipated or enacted. It is rather characterized by a new resolve on God's part. That resolve is that:

- Jerusalem will be the new center and rallying point for the assembly of the world's peoples (4:1–2).[14]
- They will assemble in Jerusalem for Torah instruction (v. 2).
- YHWH will be established and recognized as the umpire of justice between the nations (v. 3).
- The nations, in response to Torah teaching, will undertake disarmament (v. 3).
- The new adherents to Torah will settle for a modest standard of living (vine and fig tree), in recognition of the fact that a selfindulgent standard of living evokes war (v. 4).
- There will be acknowledgement of the reality and legitimacy of "other gods," without yielding on Israel's loyalty to Yahweh (v. 5).

It is evident that this poetic scenario contradicts everything about the established reality of Jerusalem either in its acquisitiveness or in its destruction:

- That Jerusalem, unlike this imagined one, does not welcome the nations
- That Jerusalem, unlike this imagined one, gives others no access to Torah.

14. On the text, see Gottwald, *All the Kingdoms of the Earth*, 196–203.

- That Jerusalem, unlike this imagined one, keeps YHWH as Israel's patron, thus never as arbiter.

- That Jerusalem, unlike this imagined one, is fully armed with no energy for disarmament.

- That Jerusalem, unlike this imagined one, craves an extravagant standard of indulgence.

- That Jerusalem, unlike this imagined one, gives no credit or legitimacy to any other god.

The poem offers the stunning reality (a) that the listeners are placed in deep contradiction between the city given by dominant ideology and the one announced in this promissory oracle and (b) that the contradiction is sponsored and vouched for by YHWH, who is the source of the alternative. That contradiction, then, invites the listeners to choose, and to affirm that an alternative choice is possible. Thus the intent of the prophetic "performance" is that the listeners might sign on to an alternative imagination and act accordingly. At the very least, this oracle challenges and seeks to subvert and displace the Jerusalem offered by acquisitive interests.

Isaiah 65:17–25

This prophetic oracle is at the extreme edge of Old Testament hope and is a remarkable act of imagination. We may suppose that, like the sequence suggested for the Micah oracle, this oracle is offered in response to loss and lament. The book of Isaiah works in much larger scope than the tradition of Micah. But there is no doubt that the oracles of judgment in the Isaiah tradition characterize, like Micah, an urban economy engaged in self-destruction through its limitless greed (see, for example, Isa 3:1—4:1; 5:7, 8–10). Nor is there any doubt that at the center of the book of Isaiah, between chapters 39 and 40, we are to entertain the destruction of the city and the utterance of the book of Lamentations. (It is widely seen that the poetry of Isaiah 40–55, in some detail, can be heard as a response to the laments in the book of Lamentations.)[15] After chapter 40, the book of Isaiah moves to new possibility, imagining homecoming and restoration of the city.[16] But the Jerusalem to which there will be return is not the old city. It

---

15. See Willey, *Remember the Former Things*.
16. Recovery and homecoming are given full, imaginative play in Isaiah 60–62 that

is a "new Jerusalem" that matches the anticipated "new heaven" and "new earth."

- The new city here imagined will no longer be a venue for "the sound of weeping and "the cry of distress," the kind of weeping and cries that arise in situations of suffering and pain imposed by greed (v. 19).[17]
- The new city here imagined will not be a venue for infant mortality, because the life of everyone, including newborn children, will be valued and protected by policy (v. 20).
- The new city here imagined will not be a place where folk die too soon, for even the old will be valued and protected (v. 20).
- The new city here imagined will be a place for neighborly economics in which there will not be foreclosure on one's home or the right of eminent domain in the interest of the elite (vv. 21–22).
- The new city here imagined will be a venue for healthy, joyous childbirth, for the old curse linked to childbirth will no longer pertain; all the newborn will be blessed (v. 23).
- The new city here imagined will be in the constant protective purview of Yahweh, without the deep void produced by an "unclean people" (v. 24).
- The new city here imagined will be a place of reconciled "nature," because all creatures will be beyond the reach of hurt and destruction (v. 25).

It is clear that the city imagined by the traditions of Micah and Isaiah is one where human flourishing is attainable, because these poetic acts of imagination contradict the old, tired city of greed and the old, tired ideologies that continue to justify systemic greed. The listeners—the first listeners and many subsequent listeners—are invited into a contradiction where new choices are possible. As these poets know, and as the God who evokes the poets knows, it is possible to keep choosing the old, tired city of greed and to keep embracing the old, tired ideologies that justify that greed. Such a choice, however, is not required. The work of the poem is to break the totalism of that ideology of greed—not to deliver the listener into a panacea,

conjure a wondrous, triumphant return.

17. On the cry, see Boyce, *The Cry to God in the Old Testament*.

but into a context where alternatives are chooseable. "Flourishing" is not a given; but it is made chooseable.

The Hard Work of Imagination

The work of such poetic imagination is to dislodge the "givenness" of the claims of acquisitive ideology. If that givenness is dislodged, then alternatives become thinkable and chooseable. My thesis is that the hard work of imagination (that claims divine rootage and divine propulsion) is a fundamental precondition for a society that can flourish. The sad reality of our contemporary society is that the possible venues for such imagination (that is rooted in and propelled by holiness out beyond the reach of human hubris)—perhaps the university, more likely the church or synagogue, or the mosque—have largely succumbed to the dictates of acquisitiveness that are disguised as virtues. The possibility of such imagination pivots on God-authorized contradiction that requires a kind of courageous intentionality that is not possible among those who deny or despair.

The hopeful reality is that Micah and Isaiah, in that ancient world, are not the last such voices of imagination that continue to echo. In the United States, there is no more dramatic instance of such imaginative public utterance that bespeaks flourishing than "I Have a Dream" by Martin Luther King Jr.[18] His use of "dream" seems to me to be a cagey, judicious way of claiming theological rootage in a society that is doubtful of such rootage, for "dream" is a world beyond managed memo, a world haunted by the spirit of truth beyond our weary categories.[19] Thus King speaks of "dream" and in fact lines out a particular, concrete alternative for society that the dream treats as possible.

It is clear in the cadences of his speech that he intends, point by point, to contradict the assumptions and practices of a racist society of greed and exploitation. Thus: "All men are created equal" defies racist hierarchy; "sons of former slaves and sons of former slave owners" refuses racist distinctions; "sweltering with the heat of injustice and oppression" acknowledges the unbearable burden of old practices. And so on, point by point. King's

---

18. King, "I Have a Dream," 404–6.

19. In Isa 2:1, the offer of an alternative Jerusalem is termed a "vision." It is suggestive that in the familiar "Holy City," the lyric begins: "Last night as I lay sleeping, / I had a dream so fair . . ." Perhaps the new Jerusalem, like the new America offered by King, is always a "dream."

speech is in close proximity to the promissory utterances of Micah and Isaiah. It is an act of hope. Clearly, however, it is also a summons to act toward possibility. That speech contributed—as intended and, as it turned out, in an effective way—to the passage of the crucial Civil Rights legislation of the decade. The speech named, exposed, and called out a society that vigorously refused self-criticism and self-awareness, and invited King's listeners into the heretofore unnamed contradiction between practice and creed. King ended his "oracle" with a riff on "Let freedom ring," a phrase from a beloved anthem, "My Country 'Tis of Thee." Without it being said, every listener knew that he meant not only life in new freedom, but also freedom from old, killing assumptions. The "ring of freedom" requires action; but it begins in the poetry of flourishing.

Emancipatory Imagination

So now the United States (and the Western world with it) faces choices that are more difficult and demanding, even, than those of race, for economics is the toughest case. The possibility is that the old ideologies of acquisitiveness, birthed in coercive monologue and sustained by aggressive militarism, may be "dreamed" away. That will require emancipatory imagination, that is, poets who live and speak beyond the totalism of accepted truth. Poets of all sorts—artists, preachers, intellectuals, and ordinary folk who know better—have been in a long season of intimidation with failed nerve.[20] But pain may produce such poetry. And this may be such a time. Pain-produced poetry evokes communities that imagine alternatively and that initiate action that is both subversive and generative. Such flourishing is possible, granted God-given nerve. And when it is sounded among us, we will notice, yet again, how much Tim Gorringe has taught us so well.

---

20. On such a condition, see Friedman, *A Failure of Nerve*.

Bibliography

Boyce, Richard Nelson. *The Cry to God in the Old Testament*. SBLDS 103. Atlanta: Scholars, 1988.

Brueggemann, Walter. "Psalms 9–10: A Counter to Conventional Social Reality." In *The Bible and the Politics of Exegesis: Essays in Honor of Norman K. Gottwald on His Sixty-Fifth Birthday*, edited by David Jobling et al., 3–15. Cleveland: Pilgrim, 1991.

———. *Solomon: Israel's Ironic Icon of Human Achievement*. Studies on Personalities of the Old Testament. Columbia: University of South Carolina Press, 2005.

Cavanaugh, William T. *Torture and Eucharist: Theology, Politics, and the Body of Christ*. Challenges in Contemporary Theology. Oxford: Blackwell, 1998.

Friedman, Edwin H. *A Failure of Nerve: Leadership in the Age of the Quick Fix*. Bethesda, MD: Edwin Friedman Estate/Trust, 1999.

Gorringe, Timothy J. *Capital and the Kingdom: Theological Ethics and Economic Order*. Maryknoll, NY: Orbis, 1994.

———. *Harvest: Food, Farming and the Churches*. London: SPCK, 2006.

Gottwald, Norman K. *All the Kingdoms of the Earth: Israelite Prophecy and International Relations in the Ancient Near East*. 1964. Reprinted, Minneapolis: Fortress, 2008.

Jacques, Martin. *When China Rules the World: The End of the Western World and the Birth of a New Global Order*. New York: Penguin, 2009.

Johnson, Chalmers. *Blowback: The Costs and Consequences of American Empire*. New York: Metropolitan, 2001.

———. *Nemesis: The Last Days of the American Republic*. New York: Metropolitan, 2006.

———. *The Sorrows of Empire: Militarism, Secrecy, and the End of the Republic*. New York: Metropolitan, 2005.

King, Martin Luther, Jr. "I Have a Dream." In *Sociology of Religion: A Reader*, edited by Susanne C. Monahan et al., 404–6. Upper Saddle River, NJ: Prentice-Hall, 2001.

Miller, Patrick D. *They Cried to the Lord: The Form and Theology of Biblical Prayer*. Minneapolis: Fortress, 1994.

Walzer, Michael. *Exodus and Revolution*. New York: Basic, 1985.

Wilder, Amos Niven. *Theopoetic: Theology and the Religious Imagination*. 1976. Reprinted, Eugene, OR: Wipf & Stock, 2013.

Willey, Patricia Tull. *Remember the Former Things: The Recollection of Previous Texts in Second Isaiah*. SBLDS 161. Atlanta: Scholars, 1997.

Žižek, Slavoj. *The Universal Exception*. Edited by Rex Butler and Scott Stephens. New York: Continuum, 2006.

5

A Royal Miracle and Its *Nachleben*

Good years of collegiality and team-teaching have left me greatly indebted to Doug Meeks.[1] The only way I can think to acknowledge that debt is to offer a reading of a text that I hope and intend to be congruent with an interpretive perspective that I have learned from him.

The Elisha Narratives

The books of First and Second Kings consists in forty-seven chapters that trace the Davidic monarchy in Jerusalem from the death of David to the fall of Jerusalem, perhaps 962–587 BCE, plus a paragraph perhaps added some years later (2 Kgs 25:27–30). That long royal recital is largely formulaic, including a verdict of "good king" or "bad king," a judgment commonly attributed to the Deuteronomist, that is, a theological judgment based on the theology of the tradition of the book of Deuteronomy. Alongside that recital the text traces the unstable royal dynasties of northern Israel from the schism of 922 to the fall of the northern capitol of Samaria in 722 at the hands of the Assyrians. The substance of the books is a roster of established power, what scholars would now term "the urban elite" who lived off the produce and wealth generated by peasant agriculture, extracted from them by the well organized tax system, on which see 1 Kgs 4:7–19. The formulaic report pauses only occasionally for narrative episodes, notably concerning Solomon (1 Kings 3–11), Joash (2 Kings 11), Hezekiah (2 Kings 18–20), and Josiah (2 Kings 22–23). The plot line proceeds on the assumption that

---

1. My debts to Blair Meeks are comparably great. In a formal introduction for lecture by Elisabeth Moltmann-Wendel, Blair puckishly added, "Her husband Jürgen is a fine theologian in his own right." So also in Blair's presence, her husband, Doug, is a fine theologian in his own right.

the recital of kings constitutes the normative account of the history of Israel and Judah, an assumption that has been largely shared in modern interpretation. The equation of "office holders" and "history" is of course a common assumption among us, given in our memorization of "the kings and queens of England" or the US presidents, a memory that is often supplemented by the list of wars that have been won by the office holders, only of late recognizing as well some wars that have been lost!

The most remarkable literary datum of this forty-seven chapter chronicle is that it is abruptly and dramatically interrupted by a very different narrative, namely the accounts of the prophetic appearances of Elijah, Micaiah, and Elisha. The initial intrusion upon the "roster of power" is the appearance of Elijah in 1 Kgs 17:1:

> Now Elijah, the Tishbite, of Tishbe in Gilead said to Ahab, "As the Yahweh the God of Israel lives, before whom I stand, there shall be neither dew nor rain these years, except by my word.

Elijah receives no introduction from the narrator. He is given no pedigree and no social location, except "the Tishbite," a term that helps us not at all. Elijah receives four chapters of reportage, 1 Kgs 17–19, 21. He is followed in 1 Kings 22 (one chapter only) by Micaiah who is identified only as a "son of Imlah." He is, in the narrative, regarded by the royal office holders as an exception, thought by the king of Northern Israel to be often a bearer of bad news to the kings and therefore more likely to offer some reliable word . . . which he does not in this instance! After him comes Elisha, son of Shaphat, introduced in 1 Kgs 19:19–21, who waits until 2 Kings 2, at the ascension of Elijah, to begin his extended narrative performance. From that beginning point, he is privileged to have eight chapters of narrative 2–9, plus a belated appearance in chapter 13. The sum of the narratives concerning these prophets, Elisha, Micaiah, and Elisha, amounts to thirteen chapters, not counting the odd narrative of Elisha in 2 Kings 13. Thus these three inexplicable characters occupy *thirteen* of the *forty-seven* chapters of the royal recital, a sizable proportion of the whole.

One readily senses a remarkable disjunction in the attention given to the three. These chapters are quite unlike the formulaic royal recitals. In critical judgment they bear few marks of the Deuteronomic editing.[2] They differ radically from the royal chronicle in content and therefore in

---

2. Noth, *The Deuteronomistic History*, had seen that the prophetic narratives bear few marks of the Deuteronomic historian.

theological perspective. Those differences, moreover, are matched by a different literary articulation. The roster of establishment power is something like a *chronicle* with the tone and expression of a memo. By contrast these three receive such *narrative* presentation that scholarship readily labels their reports as "legends," a term that would not be used for royal formulae.[3] While the term "legend" is a form critical usage following Herman Gunkel, there can hardly be any doubt that such scholarly usage also means to suggest that the narratives are fanciful, propelled by playful imagination, and lacking in historical reliability. The contrast of styles is complete between royal report that has a sense of the "factual" about it and the prophetic narratives that proceed in something like playful fantasy that is surely not factually reliable.

Thus we have at the center of the books of Kings an alternative articulation that is at best irreverent toward royal power, that perhaps in its very presentation intends to be subversive of and dissenting from royal claims to authority. Consequently the books might better be entitled "Kings?" with a doubting question mark. This "hidden transcript" suggest an alternative account of history, one to which the power roster barely had access.[4] That alternative features different plot lines, different characters, and different outcomes. This account remains "hidden" only because in the ancient draft it is contained within the royal recital and because in our modern critical reading scholarship, with its tenured epistemology, has been free to disregard, dismiss, and explain away a version of history "from below" that "from above" seems hardly credible. Thus the books of Kings are put together as a staging ground for a vigorous contestation about the nature of history. Like every such contestation, this one is concerned with the truth of power.[5]

When we consider the Elisha narrative, the text that I will consider here, one is struck by the way in which royal figures are treated, if at all. They are reported in a way that contradicts the "royal recital," so that royal claims to authority are by narrative process largely deconstructed. The narrator takes his time with these interruptions and subversions of royal power. While royal memos can be summarized and routinized, subversive

---

3. Most recently Walzer, *In God's Shadow*, 80, refers to these prophets as "legendary heroes."

4. The allusion is to Scott, *Domination and the Arts or Resistance*. The royal and prophetic scripts compete in the books of Kings, but the prophetic script is "under the radar."

5. See Brueggemann, *Truth Speaks to Power*.

A Royal Miracle and Its *Nachleben*

narratives cannot be hurried. They must be relished and lingered over, careful detail by careful detail:

- In 2 Kings 4, this subversive character, Elisha, is alone with an economically bereft widow (vv. 1–7). He turns on the widow's spigot of olive oil, saves her house from foreclosure, and recovers her children about to be sold into slavery.

- In the same chapter 4, Elisha receives the defaulted body of the boy, breathes new life into him, and says, without further elaboration, "Take your son" (v. 36).

- In chapter 5, Elisha disregards the status and prestige of the general-cum-leprosy and sends him to the Jordan for recovery (v. 10). And then he sends him home to Damascus to worship his idols with only the blessing, "shalom" (v. 19).

- In chapter 6, Elisha turns out to be a player in the centuries-old Israeli-Syrian war. He prays the enemy into blindness (v. 18); then he prays the enemy back to sight after they have been captured (v. 20). He counters the old and deep hostility with a huge feast; he feeds the enemy (v. 23)! The anonymous, irrelevant king (minus the formulae of royal dignity) wants to kill the Syrians, but he is dismissed along with his thirst for vengeance by Elisha.

- Later in chapter 6 Elisha presides over an intense famine. The crisis is that, as in every famine, there is food; but in its shortage, food is too expensive for poor people to buy. The famine is ended because YHWH crated panic among the Syrians who abandoned their food supply. Yet again Elisha anticipates such food that the king is helpless to deliver.

In all of these narratives, the prophet, the interrupter of royal power, occupies center stage. He comes without status, intrudes into the royal narrative without pedigree, and enacts transformations "from below."

In this long narrative pause in the royal chronicle, the claims of royal authority are superseded. More than that, they are portrayed as foolish and without force. The king is absent amid the wonders of chapter 4. But then the king appears:

- In the healing of Naaman, the king disclaims any ability to heal:

> Am I God, to give death or life, that this man sends word to me to cure a man of leprosy? Just look and see how he is trying to pick a quarrel with me. (5:7)

- In the war with Syria, the king enters the story late, with a thirst for vengeance but without authority:

  > Father, shall I kill them (6:21)?

He is refuted by the prophet:

> No! Did you capture with your sword and your bow those whom you want to kill? (6:22)

- In the midst of the famine, the king denies the capacity to provide food:

  > No! Let the Yahweh help you. How can I help you? From the threshing floor or from the wine press?" (6:27)

That is all! Kings are not life-givers! They are portrayed as inept and impotent. For good reason the king remains unnamed in the narrative, having done nothing to merit identity or reputation.

After this series of episodes of inexplicable pastoral transformation, we come to a political coup instigated by the prophet. In chapter 9 Elisha manages a secret anointing to set in motion a revolution that will place Jehu, the zealot, on the throne in Samaria:

> When you arrive, look for Jehu, son of Jehoshaphat, son of Nimshi; go in and get him to leave his companions, and take him into an inner chamber. Then take the flask of oil, pour it on his head, and say, "Thus says Yahweh: I *anoint* you king over Israel. Then open the door and flee; do not linger." (9:2–3)

The young man dispatched by the prophet does the anointing:

> Thus says Yahweh, the God of Israel: I *anoint* you king over the people of Yahweh, over Israel; you shall strike down the house of your master Ahab, so that I may avenge on Jezebel the blood of my servants the prophets, and the blood of all the servants of Yahweh. (9:6–7)

Finally, after resisting disclosure of the treasonable act, Jehu acknowledges the act to his companions:

> This is just what he said to me: Thus says the Lord, I *anoint* you king over Israel. (9:12)

Three times the verb "anoint" is sounded, a sacramental gesture by the prophet that gives legitimacy to a social revolution. In this narrative, Elisha has moved from the pastoral to the political, now for the first time directly challenging the legitimacy of the rule of Ahab and his family. Perhaps he judges that pastoral acts are no longer enough to effect change. The action initiated by Elisha in chapter 9 is played out in violence; the death of Jezebel fulfills the anticipation of Elijah (9:3–37; see 1 Kgs 21:23). In chapter 10 a bloody elimination of the entire royal house is performed:

> So Jehu killed all who were left of the house of Ahab in Jezreel, all is leaders, close friends, and priests, until he left no survivor. (10:11)

Then comes the death, the violent death, of all those loyal to Baal and the covenant-violating social system legitimated by Baal (10:18–31). It is not a pretty picture that emerges from such determined religious absolutism!! The narrator, however, seems to have no other way to imagine regime change except by violence that is grounded in prophetic zeal. Once the prophet disrupts royal continuity, there is no telling!

2 Kings 8:1–6

Thus the Elisha narrative consists in two quite distinct arenas. In chapters 4–7, we have a series of intimate pastoral transformations. In chapters 8–10 we witness public actions of violent overthrows of power. Our interest, in what follows, is the peculiar narrative of 2 Kgs 8:1–6 that seems to mark a divider between these two narrative foci. Two points are important as we move into this narrative. On the one hand we have in chapters 4–7 a series of texts that discount the *unnamed king as inept, impotent, and irrelevant*. On the other hand in chapters 8–10 we have seen actions initiated by Elisha that have *destabilized the Northern dynasty of Ahab* and furthered rabid religious passion (also chapter 8).

It is then a surprise to find the narrative of 8:1–6 wedged between 4–7 that discounts the king and 8–10 that destabilizes kingship. We are surprised because in this narrative the king is the defining and decisive character. Though still unnamed, the king in this narrative is not inept, impotent, or irrelevant. Rather this is a king who is fully in charge and who is able to act effectively, quite in contrast to the previous articulations of the king.

This narrative opens with two recognizable themes. First the presenting problem is a famine. While the scarcity of food had been resolved in the narrative of chapters 6–7, the problem is a continuing or recurring one. Food shortages make the cost of food too expensive except for those who are privileged and powerful. The famine, moreover, is to last seven years, perhaps an echo of the old pharonic nightmare about famine (Gen 41:1–7). The crisis to come upon Israel will be acute in a way that requires emergency action.

Second, the first character presented in the narrative is recognizable, the woman "whose son he had restored to life" in chapter 4. From that earlier text we know that she had a husband (v. 25) and was wealthy (v. 8). She was, moreover, deeply devoted to Elisha, first because she had shown him hospitality (vv. 10–11), and second, because he had restored her son to life (vv. 35–36).

But now in chapter 8, this same woman is in a very different circumstance. First, there is no mention of her husband; perhaps she is now a widow that makes her more vulnerable. We are not told. Second, her previously reported wealth will not protect her in the face of the famine. She is now a person in potentially dire circumstance. In the previous story she had been "bitter" about the death of her son (4:27). Now she is advised by Elisha to flee from the famine. She does not ask Elisha to cope himself with the famine, nor does he offer such help. Here he is realistic and pragmatic: Go where there is food! She goes away—to the Philistines—for seven years! We are left to conclude, without any data, that she received adequate food during that interim period.

But the crisis upon which the narrative turns does not concern where she was among the Philistines, or even the famine. It is rather back home from which she had been absent for seven years. The narrative is terse about her return home. It assumes, but does not report, that she had lost her property. We are not told how, either simply in the rough-and-tumble of economics during her absence, or whether the king had reassigned her property to others. In any case, this once wealthy woman is now without resources. We already know from chapter 4 that she is a woman capable of public business. Here she goes to court. She lodges an "appeal" (8:3). The term "cry" here means to make a formal court complaint. But that term,

A Royal Miracle and Its *Nachleben*

even in such usage, is not without emotive power.[6] The cry—as we know both in narrative (Exod 2:23) and in commandment (Exod 22:23, 27) is a vigorous assertion that is designed to mobilize social (theological?) power to right a wrong, to correct an injustice.[7] While Elisha had counseled her at the beginning of the seven years, he is not present at her return. It is her own initiative that has led her to the royal court.

But then the narrative is interrupted. The narrator takes us inside the chamber of the king . . . still unnamed. The king is in conversation with Gehazi, Elisha's rather unsavory aide. We know him from two previous narratives. In chapter 4, he was involved with the crisis of the dead son. First, he tries to push the mother away from Elisha, perhaps to protect his master (4:22). Then he himself addresses the dead child, but to no effect (4:31). His second appearance is at the end of the Naaman episode in which he appears as an extortionist. As pay-back for his action, he is struck with leprosy (5:19–27). In both narratives, he surely is not much in sync with Elisha's self-presentation. Now in our present episode, he is chatting with the king. We not told how he gained access to the king. But his presence there may make one suspicious: his access to the royal presence might suggest a betrayal of Elisha. But the narrative does not comment. The only one who speaks in this exchange is the king who invites Gehazi to tell about Elisha's "great deeds" ("great things"). This is a most remarkable invitation. It makes evident that the king knows about Elisha's actions and is curious about them. Of course we do not know if the king's query is ironic or straight-forward. If straight-forward, the king is impressed by what he has heard of Elisha. If ironic, the king may, not unlike the cynical general in 5:11–12, belittle the performance of Elisha and imagine that in truth this uncredentialed character could not possibly do "great things."

Either way, the king uses the term "great things," a term not anywhere else used in the Elisha's narrative. The royal use of the term would seem to be an acknowledgement that Elisha has indeed performed acts that are beyond royal capacity or explanation. The term is otherwise used in the biblical text for "divine wonders," most particularly the Exodus deliverance:

> Just remember what the Lord your God did to Pharaoh and to all
> Egypt, the *great trials* that your eyes saw, the signs and wonders,

---

6. For a full exposition of "the cry," see Boyce, *The Cry to God in the Old Testament*.

7. On such mobilization of social power, see Sheppard, "'Enemies' and the Politics of Prayer in the Book of Psalms."

> the mighty hand and the outstretched arm by which the Lord your God brought you out. (Deut 7:18–19)

> He is your praise; he is your God, who has done for you these *great and awesome things* that your own eyes have seen. Your ancestors went down to Egypt seventy persons; and now the Lord your God has made you as numerous as the stars in heaven. (Deut 10:21–22; see Deut 29:3; Josh 24:17)[8]

Now the king takes that term from the Exodus tradition to refer to Elisha's narrative performance that is, each time, an act that brings new life out of deathly circumstances of leprosy, famine, and war.

Gehazi responds to the king's query, though we do not get a direct quote from him. He focuses, in his response we are told, precisely on the restoration of "a dead person to life," the episode in which Gehazi had been involved.[9] But Gehazi, in his response, is interrupted. 2 Kgs 8:5 is a curious verse. The very character who is the subject of Gehazi's narrative now appears in person. Gehazi stops his narrative and functions as a receptionist, perhaps accepting his role as an aide and not a peer to the king. His announcement of the woman may be for him a verification of his narrative rendition, as though to say to the king, "See, I told you!" Gehazi serves only to bring the woman into the king's presence; he then disappears from the account.

But now the woman is in a new posture. Now she is not primarily the woman with a dead son; now she is the woman with lost property. She has "appealed" to the king. Thus her script from v. 3 is restated before the king. She is the demanding suppliant in the royal court. She seeks restoration from the king of her property, as she had sought the redress of her son from Elisha. Her script is an insistence that she had been dealt an injustice, and only the king can give restitution. The king interviews the woman in order to get the facts of her case. Having the facts in hand, the king acts quickly and decisively. He designates a court official to oversee the case. The king never verbalizes a verdict; but his actions clearly indicate the royal judgment that an injustice has been perpetrated against the woman and must be corrected. The outcome is the royal verb, "restore," with reference to her

---

8. The only other usage in Ezek 16:61 is not relevant to our theme.

9. The linkage between historical deliverance and resurrection is given lyrical expression by Paul in Rom 4:17.

house and property. The king provides, moreover, that she receive all past revenues from her land during her seven year absence.

This brief narrative is remarkably complex, made so especially by the character of Gehazi. But the plot-line of action is not complex. It is *restoration* in response to the *appeal*. The appeal is so effective and compelling that the king immediately authorizes restoration. This royal act of restoration, however, is no obvious or sure thing. Indeed in context it is a quite remarkable act. It is remarkable and unexpected because kings (leaders of the "urban elite") are not habituated in granting petitions from lowly losers. More than that, however, we would not expect such a verdict from an heir of Ahab. We would not expect in on two counts. First, we would not expect it because, as chapters 9–10 indicate, the Ahab dynasty consists in practitioners of Baalism, a practice that is not only religious but that has socio-economic implications that are imperious to justice claims. More than that, we would not expect it because the king's act is a dramatic contradiction of Ahab's (and Jezebel's) action concerning Naboth's vineyard that runs roughshod over old claims of property as heritage.[10] In this case, the king acts against such confiscatory policies that enjoy religious legitimacy.

We may thus puzzle about how this "great thing" might have happened. I dare to suggest that the king's awareness of Elisha's work and his "great things," about which the king knows, provides in the text an unacknowledged impetus and motivation for the king. It is credible to think that the king could recognize that Elisha' restorative performance constituted a challenge to a dynasty that did not do restoration. The king, I suggest, is challenged enough by the prophetic witness that he himself must move out of his socio-economic narcoticism to establish himself as capable of restorative acts. The consequence is a "great thing" enacted by the king. This is a "royal miracle" that comes in the wake of the prophetic miracles. I entertain the thought that there was a kind of "contagion" in the Elisha witness to social possibility that summons the king to act out beyond the conventions of the dynasty.[11] Neither Gehazi nor the narrator comments, and the king is quite terse. But the outcome is an *answered appeal* in which the vulnerable woman receives back what is rightly hers.

10. It occurs to me that this restoration of land is an exact counterpoint to the "take possession" of Ahab and Jezebel in 1 Kings 21.

11. A compelling example of such "contagion" is the case of F. W. De Klerk in South Africa, who finally engaged the "great things" of Nelson Mandela, perhaps helped along by the witness of Desmond Tutu and the various church leaders who clustered around the *Kairos Document*.

The Parables of Jesus

The Elijah–Elisha narratives linger in the imagination of Israel. They linger as a paradigm for the disruption of worldly power by the elusive power of God that is characteristically enacted by human agents "from below." Such a way of articulating subversive power serves the Gospel narrative in the Christian tradition with regard to John the Baptist and then with regard to Jesus. As Tom Brodie has shown, there cannot be any doubt that the Elijah-Elisha narratives have an important afterlife in the imagination of the Gospel writers.[12] To be sure, this pertains principally to Elijah and much less to Elisha. And indeed the reference to 2 Kings 5 and the healing Naaman in Luke 4:27 is the only explicit reference to Elisha in the New Testament. It would not surprise us, however, to have less direct allusions to the Elisha narrative in the church's imagination.

In what follows I consider the probability that the parable by Jesus in Luke 18:1-8 is an important evidence of the afterlife of our narrative from 2 Kgs 8:1-6. The parable is situated in Jesus' instruction to his disciples about prayer that concerns not "losing heart" (v. 1). After the parable of vv. 2-5, the interpretive reflection of vv. 6-8 concern:

- The verdict of the *unjust* judge;
- A rhetorical question concerning God's grant of *justice*; a question that requires "yes" as an answer;
- The agency of the ones who *cry out* in their chosenness;
- The answer in verse 8 to the rhetorical question of verse 7 concerning God's *justice*.

The text teems with "justice," the cry for justice, and the gift of justice. The final question turns the question of justice to a question of faith. Faith is confidence in God's readiness to do justice. That confidence to pray (cry) for justice is a refusal to "lose heart." Thus prayer is not merely an act of petition; it is rather an elemental confidence that God does indeed do justice in response to cry.

The parable itself features a widow who petitions for justice so long that she wearied the judge.[13] A desperate *widow* in need of *justice* who

---

12. Brodie, *The Crucial Bridge*.

13. Note the alternative translation as given in NRSV: "so that she may not finally come and slap me in the face."

files *appeal* sounds much like a replay of the woman in 2 Kings 8. There she is not identified as a widow, but she has, in the story, no mentioned husband. She pushes her way into the court of the king with her petition. In the parable the counterpart to the woman is a judge "who neither fears God nor had respect for persons." The unnamed king in 2 Kings 8 is not characterized in that negative way; but the description of "unjust" might have fit Ahab, his father, and might, in anticipation, be used to describe Ahab's son as well. We have no single hint ahead of time that the unnamed king is not unjust like his father and like that belated unjust judge. There is no reason, in the older text, to expect the king (as a final judge) to grant justice to the woman. In the same way there is no reason to expect that the cynical judge in the parable would grant justice to the woman. In both cases, *the cry from below* impinges upon the authority figure in unexpected ways. In the parable the judge relents of his cynicism because of the relentlessness of the petitioning widow.

In the older text we are not told why the king rules in her favor. But the only factor that is of interest in the narrative is testimony to Elisha and his "great things" that restore life in a community of desperate need. In the older text, the unnamed king commits a "royal miracle," "royal" in that it is the work of the king, "miracle" because it is completely counter-intuitive that the king would grant restoration to the woman. It is impossible, in my judgment, to imagine this "royal miracle" except in the context of the prophetic miracles of restoration to which Gehazi witnesses.

In the appeal, the ruling of the judge is no less a "miracle," thus a judicial miracle. It is a miracle because it is against all odds and violates all the protocols of conventional power and conventional justice. Thus Jesus is summoning his disciples to be bold, confident, counter-intuitively confident that the world that appears closed in indifferent power is potentially open to restorative miracles, made open by the incessant prayer from below that is relentless and without doubt. The miracle of the king, like the later miracle of the judge in the parable, is not "supernatural." It is conducted by a human agent, in this case the judge, in the earlier case by the king. My judgment is that the parable is richer in depth and intensity when it is recognized as a reperformance of the older narrative in which the voice of the cry holds the upper hand over settled power that possesses the gift of justice.

The Transfiguraton of Politics

In the sequence that I have pursued—a) the Elisha narratives; b) the narrative of 2 Kgs 8:1–6; and c) the parable of Jesus—we have nothing less than a "Transfiguration of Politics" that is inevitably at the same time a transfiguration of religion.[14] In both the texts in 2 Kings and Luke, the formidable representative of establishment power is clear. In Kings, it is the sequence of Davidic rulers, even though our narrative concerns the impressive dynasty of Omri in the North. In the Gospel narrative, the power structure is fully identified in the tradition of Luke:

> In the fifteenth year of the reign of Emperor Tiberius, when Pontius Pilate was governor of Judea, and Herod was ruler of Galilee, and his brother Philip ruler of the region of Ituraea and Trachonitus, and Lysanias ruler of Abilene, during the high priesthood of Annas and Caiaphas. (Luke 3:1–2)

But the narrative of royal/imperial power is each time disrupted. As it is disrupted by Elijah and Elisha in the books of Kings, so it was disrupted in the Gospel narrative by John the Baptizer and by Jesus. And now in the parable, the disciples are summoned to be continuing disruptors of settled power that is self-serving and so biased against justice for those below:

- The narratives of Elisha and Elisha attest that the royal narrative is capable of interruption. Again and again, the Elisha narrative attests to the dysfunction and therefore the irrelevance of royal power. In 2 Kings 8, it is as though for an instant, under the tutelage of Elisha, this heir of Ahab comes to awareness and acts against royal protocol for the sake of the petitioning woman that is in front of him. He does a "great thing"!

- The parable of Jesus, an echo of that older narrative, exhibits the way in which judicial power, surely authorized by king or by empire, can be interrupted for the sake of justice. The unjust judge does a "great thing"! Even the rules of the empire (of the "Medes and Persians") are vulnerable to the cry from below when it is loud and long enough (see Dan 6:8, 15)![15]

---

14. The phrase is from Paul Lehmann, *The Transfiguration of Politics*. Lehmann's argument continues to be pertinent among us.

15. In the concluding doxology of Dan 6:27, the Living God is praised who "works signs and wonders." With different words we again hear witness concerning "great things" that defy the "unchanging" rule of the empire.

- But the parable is a parable. It is parabolic witness to the way of God. "Prayer" may be addressed to a king who belongs to the family of Ahab or to a judge authorized by Rome. But at the end, prayer is addressed to God who, in response to the cry, will "quickly grant justice."

Thus all "systems of power" are penetratable in heaven and on earth. None of them is settled, closed, and fixed. It is only those "above" who want to imagine that it is all settled, closed, and fixed and who, by ideological practice, recruit those "below" into that despairing conviction. In the end, however, those "below" know better. This is the "hidden transcript" that refuses to accept the public transcript from above.[16]

When I worked on this I had on my mind the matter of "class warfare," a slogan that now recurs in our political life. It is ironic (or predictable!) that that accusatory phrase is most often on the lips of those "above" who accuse those below of "advocating class warfare." By that they mean calling attention the socio-economic inequities that they want to keep concealed under the guise that "we are all in this together." This guise gives cover, characteristically, to the continued "class warfare" that is steadily but surreptitiously conducted from above. Given the category of class warfare, it may be argued that all of these "interruptions" of royal narrative (in Kings and in the Gospel) are exactly practices of class warfare, calling 11attention the discrepancies of power and possibility that must be redressed.[17] By transposing the issue of justice into the issue of faith in Luke 18:8, Jesus' teaching concerns courage, confidence, and resolve to continue the cry from below in the conviction that all of the injustices perpetrated by kings, by empire, and by God are transfigurable.

There must be some irony in the fact that in Luke 18 this robust teaching on prayer is followed by another parable that culminates with the prayer, "God be merciful to me a sinner" (v. 13). That latter is the prayer much preferred in a church that colludes with settled power. Surely the parable in vv. 3–5 is an alternative to too much "humbling." It is likely that Gehazi, who observed the "royal miracle" in its performance, would have seen the cogency of the more demanding prayer. The insistent claim of these texts is that God can indeed respond with wonders; beyond that, however, it is that

---

16. For utilization of the categories of James C. Scott to biblical texts, see Horsley, ed., *Hidden Transcripts and the Arts of Resistance*.

17. Hedges, *Death of the Liberal Class*, 17, has averred, "Hope will come with the return of the language of class conflict and rebellion, language that has been purged from the lexicon of the liberal class."

establishment human agents can perform miracles that violate seemingly settled royal protocols. Such faith attests that justice will out!

Bibliography

Boyce, Richard Nelson. *The Cry to God in the Old Testament.* SBLDS 103. Atlanta: Scholars, 1988.

Brodie, Thomas L. *The Crucial Bridge: The Elijah–Elisha Narrative as an Interpretive Synthesis of Genesis–Kings and a Literary Model for the Gospels.* Collegeville, MN: Liturgical, 2000.

Brueggemann, Walter. *Truth Speaks to Power: The Counter-Cultural Nature of Scripture.* Louisville: Westminster John Knox, 2013.

Hedges, Chris. *Death of the Liberal Class.* New York: Nation Books, 2010.

Horsley, Richard A., ed. *Hidden Transcripts and the Arts of Resistance: Applying the Work of James C. Scott to Jesus and Paul.* Semeia Studies 48. Atlanta: Society of Biblical Literature, 2004.

Lehmann, Paul. *The Transfiguration of Politics: The Presence and Power of Jesus of Nazareth in and over Human Affairs.* New York: Harper & Row, 1975.

Noth, Martin. *The Deuteronomistic History.* JSOTSup 15. Sheffield: JSOT Press, 1981.

Scott, James C. *Domination and the Arts or Resistance: Hidden Transcripts.* New Haven: Yale University Press, 1990.

Sheppard, Gerald T. "'Enemies' and the Politics of Prayer in the Book of Psalms." In *The Bible and the Politics of Exegesis: Essays in Honor of Norman K. Gottwald on His Sixty-Fifth Birthday*, edited by David Jobling et al., 61–82. Cleveland: Pilgrim, 1991.

Walzer, Michael. *In God's Shadow: Politics in the Hebrew Bible.* New Haven: Yale University Press, 2012.

6

The Living Afterlife of a Dead Prophet: Words that Keep Speaking

John Holbert, happily, is alive and well. He is getting old, but he is not dead. The discussion that follows concerns a dead prophet, one who stays alive even in his death.

Continuing Effective Power for Life

Elisha had a vigorous ministry, both public and pastoral. It concludes, according to the biblical text with his instigation of a political coup in 2 Kgs 9:1. After that we hear no more from him except for his odd encounter with King Joash (2 Kgs 13:14–19) and the even more curious note of 2 Kgs 13:20–21 that is the subject of this discussion. In these two terse final verses (usually ignored by the commentaries), it is reported:

- that Elisha died and was buried;
- that another man was being buried later;
- that due to pressure from a "marauding band" (presumably of Moabites) the second dead man was thrown into Elisha's grave.

We are not told why that action was taken; perhaps it was to protect the corpse from abuse at the hands of thugs. In any case,

- when the corpse "touched the bones of Elisha," he was restored to life.

This report is readily slotted as an "anecdote" to go along with much of the Elisha narrative that is "legend." One must, nevertheless, wonder why the narrative is there. My assumption and the basis for what follows in this discussion is that the "miracle of resurrection" enacted by contact with the bones of the dead prophet is to indicate that the prophet still has continuing effective power for life, even after he is dead. That is, is body is "radioactive" and continues to emit energy for life even dead, the kind of active energy evident in the report of Jesus who was "immediately aware that power had gone forth from him" (Mark 5:30; Luke 8:46). This report on Elisha has set me to thinking, in the context of John Holbert's work, of the durable life-giving force of prophetic word and act. I wish to develop that thought in two directions concerning two primary genres of prophetic speech, the kind that "prophetic preaching" engages in only carefully and gingerly.

Indictment and Sentence

The primary genre of prophetic speech in the eighth to seventh century is the "speech of judgment" that consists in an *indictment* for actions of failed obedience and *sentence* that states the God-given judgment on the basis of the indictment.[1] The speech of judgment derives from and is based on the old covenant rhetoric of *commandment* and *sanction (blessing or curse)*. (It is because of common ignorance about the structure of covenant faith that prophetic speeches of judgment are nearly impossible in the contemporary church).

From among the many prophetic speeches of judgment I here focus on an oracle of Jeremiah offered twice in the text. In Jer 6:13–15, the speech of judgment is voiced as *indictment* (vv. 13–15a) and *sentence* (v. 15b). (See the same words in 8:10–12 where the elements of the speech are inverted.) The indictment in the poem traces self-serving leadership (v. 13) followed by false assurances of *shalom* (v. 14), leading to a verdict of "shamelessness" without being "ashamed," no longer having a capacity to blush in embarrassment. The poem characterizes a people so morally numb or cynical that it is no longer embarrassed about its deep moral failure. The sentence, introduced with a characteristic "therefore," anticipates "fall, punishment, overthrow."

Here I focus on that inability to feel shame because our moral sensibility has been overcome by aggressive greed sustained by deception. The focus on "shame" goes beneath guilt and juridical categories to the most intimate measure of social sensibility.[2] There is no doubt that Jeremiah spoke this poetry at a time and place in the political-military crisis of Jerusalem

---

1. Westermann, *Basic Forms of Prophetic Speech*.
2. Erikson, "The Problem of Ego Identity."

that he re-imagines as a moral crisis, that is, the inability to discern public reality with reference to the covenantal expectations of YHWH. That much is uncontested in critical study.

With reference to the radioactive bones of Elisha, I propose we may go beyond critical questions to see that the poetic speech of the prophet (twice remembered in 2 Kings 6 and 8) continues to have a life well beyond immediate context. The ancient words, like the ancient bones, continue with vitality in subsequent social remembering and reflection concerning subsequent moral insensitivity. I can think of three instances in which "they do not know how to blush" continues to be a vital utterance in a community of moral reflection:

- In his great Stanford lectures, Abraham Heschel cites "a sense of ultimate embarrassment" as the ground for praise:

  > Religion depends on what man does with his ultimate embarrassment. It is the awareness that the world is too great for him, the awareness of the grandeur and mystery of being, the awareness of being present at the unfolding of an inconceivable eternal saga. Embarrassment is the awareness of a incongruity of character and challenge, of perceptivity and reality, of knowledge and understanding, of mystery and comprehension . . . It is a protection against . . . arrogance, hybris, self-deification. The end of embarrassment would be the end of humanity.[3]

- In the "McCarthy hearings," when Senator Joseph McCarthy was near the end of his nefarious career, the pixie-like attorney, Joseph Welch, asked him before the cameras, "Senator, have you at long last no shame?" Clearly the answer was, "No, no shame."

- Mayor Richard J. Daly (Chicago), caught in a profound political scandal, was asked at a press conference if he was embarrassed to be caught. His answer was, "Nothing embarrasses us."

I submit that the ancient utterance of Jeremiah keeps ringing in our ears, keeps offering vitality to evoke sensibility. We keep reading and pondering old texts, now in a context of napalm or torture in order to face the moral numbness of our culture. Perhaps Heschel, Welch, and Daly could have said all of this without the antecedent poetry of Jeremiah. But I doubt it. The words live and wait to be uttered and heard always again. In his

---

3. Heschel, *Who Is Man?*, 112–13.

"moral history of the twentieth century," Jonathan Glover writes of the "Residue of Moral Identity; Embarrassment." He takes up the hard case of the Nazi death camps and observes that they were kept hidden:

> It was fear of embarrassment, together with the fear of a public outcry, which led to policies of concealment . . . Hitler and his circle did not like to be exposed to what their policies did to people. Even they could be embarrassed . . . Even the top Nazis could feel the pressure of social disapproval. Perhaps even the top Nazis sometimes felt awkwardness, linked to the residue of an older moral identity. They tried to conceal the murder of the Jews.[4]

We may follow the judgment of Erik Erikson that shame is an elemental human awareness. The remarkable realization is that "shame" can be eradicated by sufficient moral callousness. But prophetic utterance makes that elemental awareness palpably available even in contexts where it has been forfeited. It is the hope of such utterance that the old bones and the old words can "live again."[5]

New Possibility in the Midst of Despair

The second genre of prophetic utterance is the oracle of promise that is richly offered in the sixth century, in the midst of exilic displacement.[6] Paul Hanson, in the wake of Gerhard von Rad, has summarized the way in which Israelite religion engaged in "reapplication" of older tradition to turn old memories to new interpretive possibility.[7] In a season of hopelessness, the poets grounded hope in the promissory utterances of YHWH.

Here I focus on only one text, the lyrical promise of Isa 65:17–25 concerning a new heaven, a new earth, and a new Jerusalem. What strikes one about this most extreme and sweeping promise in the Old Testament is that it focuses on real human socioeconomic issues for a time to come . . . infant mortality (v. 20), protection of private property (vv. 21–22), childbirth (v. 23), and the environment (v. 25). The poem is, moreover, a lyrical utterance of possibility that the world has long since declared to be impossible. There

---

4. Glover, *Humanity*, 353–54.

5. I refer to Ezek 37:1–14. "The Valley of Dry Bones" makes a nice counterpoint to the bones of Elisha in our text. In both cases, the wonderment is that the old, dead bones can live again . . . by the power of God.

6. See Westermann, *Prophetic Oracles of Salvation in the Old Testament*.

7. P. D. Hanson, "Israelite Religion in the Early Postexilic Period."

can be little doubt of the historical location of this utterance, and scholars are generally agreed about a post-exilic venue for this lyrical articulation among Jewish poets who refused despair.

But of course the poetry would not stay still in that ancient context. Like the living bones, this lyrical poetry has kept surging toward new possibility in seasons of great disappointment and despair. As we are all aware, the New Testament utterance with a reflection on this poetry is the large anticipation of the church when Christ becomes all in all:

> Then I saw a new heaven and a new earth; for the first heaven and firsts earth had passed away, and the sea was no more. And I saw the holy city, the new Jerusalem, coming down out of heaven from God, prepared as a bride adorned for her husband. And I heard a loud voice from the throne saying,
>
>> See, the home of God is among mortals.
>> He will dwell with them;
>> They will be his peoples,
>> And God himself will be with them;
>> he will wipe away every tear from their eyes.
>> Death will be no more;
>> Mourning and crying and pain will be no more,
>> For the first things have passed away.
>> And the one who was seated on the throne said,
>> "See, I am making all things new." (Rev 21:1–5a)

Surely it is clear that the capacity of John to offer such a vision is based in the old poetry that continues in evocative vitality. It was, moreover, that ancient lyric that invited Christians under assault to trust in God's sure future and not give in to the brutal present tense. But of course the poetry pushes out beyond the canon. Perhaps the most distinctive generativity from that poem of Isaiah (or that sort of poem) is the great Washington DC speech of Martin Luther King, "I have a dream." The "dream" is indeed a God-given vision of what God will yet give that the world judges impossible. Like ancient Isaiah, King had no idea about how to get from here to there. But the poem, on credible lips, does its own work and generates its own future, in this case not least the great Civil Rights Acts that followed.

King stands in a long line of echoes from ancient Isaiah:

> I have a dream that one day on the red hills of Georgia the sons of former slaves and sons of former slave owners will be able to sit down together at the table of brotherhood.
>
> I have a dream that one day even the state of Mississippi, a desert that swelters with the heat of injustice and oppression, will be transformed into an oasis of freedom and justice.
>
> I have a dream that my four little children will one day live in a nation where they will not be judged by the color of their skin but by the content of their character.
>
> I have a dream today...
>
> Let freedom ring from the snowcapped Rockies of Colorado!
> Let freedom ring from the curvaceous peaks of California!
> But not only that; let freedom ring from Stone Mountain of Georgia!
> Lee freedom ring from Lookout Mountain of Tennessee!
> Let freedom ring from every hill and molehill of Mississippi.
> From every mountainside, let freedom ring.[8]

There is no doubt that King's echoing speech invited (and continues to invite) his listeners out beyond present circumstance to new historical capabilities. The cadences of that speech, moreover, continue to evoke, empower, and energize. It is no wonder that Bruce Feiler can hear King's speech as a reiteration of all the great utterances of the US drama of freedom:

> His talk wove together many of the iconic themes from the 350-year merger of the Hebrew Bible and America. He evokes the Pilgrims: "Land where my fathers died, land of the Pilgrims' pride." He paid tribute to Lincoln and his use of Psalm 90: "Five score years ago, a great American, in whose symbolic shadow we stand together, signed the Emancipation Proclamation." ... In what is arguably the most famous speech by an American since the Gettysburg Address, Martin Luther King fused together Jefferson and Lincoln, Pilgrim and slave, Emma Lazarus and the Old State House bell, to set up his defining message from that "Old Negro spiritual" that Zora Neale Hurston had put into the mouths of the Israelites as they set out for the Promised land: "Free at last! Free at last! Thank God Almighty, we are free at last!"[9]

And the beat goes on!

---

8. The speech has been reprinted in many contexts; see King, "I Have a Dream."
9. Feiler, *America's Prophet*, 251–52.

The Living Afterlife of a Dead Prophet

Prophetic Speech and the Lectionary

My thought, in this exposition, is that prophetic preaching, as we undertake that task, is not only a momentary act of courage, though it is that. Much more, it is enlistment in cadences speech that reach back to Jeremiah and Isaiah, that travel with Heschel and Welch and King, and that alight for an instant in our own time and place. This practice of utterance is not unlike the bones of Elisha. Any preacher may hope to stumble into the grave of Elisha, or into the cadences of Jeremiah and Isaiah. On many days we stumble in and come to the lively bones, but are not activated, because often we are in denial or in despair; we are at the edge of silence; or we are too timed to speak. But then the old words energize, and we dare speak again, because the old words on our lips are live words, crafted afresh so that they become our own words of truth-telling.

Prophetic passages that appear in the lectionary are ordinarily treated in rather ad hoc fashion and are fairly sparse in usage and in the lectionary. But consider these texts when they are carriers of radioactive energy in a way that has vitality:

Amos 7:7–14 (Year B, Proper 10). This text features a confrontation between prophetic utterance that anticipates social dislocation and the established authority of the priest of the sanctuary who seeks to silence, because such truth-telling is more than can be borne. The text narrates the interaction of a daring risk of truth-telling and a society that resists such truth. The text invites the bold preacher to wonder what truth can be said, what truth needs to be heard in "the establishment," and what the costs of such truth-telling might be. There is no doubt that the regime of Jeroboam had created such a "bubble" of misperception that the truth sounded strange, even as it does now when uttered on our contemporary bubble of self-deception. Every truth-teller comes in the wake of Amos who declared that the establishment is penultimate and will be displaced.

Micah 5:2–5a (Year C, Fourth Sunday of Advent) voices a prophetic hope and a prophetic longing. It addresses little Bethlehem, the vulnerable village that is pitted not only against the Jerusalem establishment that Micah critiqued, but against the coming onslaught of Assyria. Bethlehem of course is the birthplace of David, and so the poem links the village to the great promises of the Davidic house that issued in messianism. The poem anticipates a new David who will come and act as the great shepherd-king who will assure peace to the villages, even in the face of the empire. The poem is of course drawn, in Christian usage, toward the birth and ministry of Jesus. Beyond that, however, is the prophetic conviction that God raises up human agents who can turn the course of history, even in the face of deep, brutal power. When all else fails for the vulnerable villagers, the prophets fall back on to poetic hope that refuses to give in to the circumstance on the ground.

Zephaniah 3:14–20 (Year C, Third Sunday of Advent). The poem is a summons to Jerusalem, that is, to all Israel, to sing and dance and celebrate, because the "real king," YHWH, is coming among the dislocated, even in a situation of enormous social, political stress. It is anticipated that this new rule of God, after a spasm of imperial abuse, will reverse the course of history and cause well-being for Jerusalem. The coming intrusion of God will "give victory," "renew you," "remove disaster," "deal with your oppressors," and "gather the lame and outcast." All of that is summed up in the final phrase of the poem, "restore your fortunes." That phrase is used repeatedly for the end of exile and the wondrous homecoming of displaced people. The poem imagines the "direct rule" of YHWH, though clearly the poet anticipates a human agent who will do this work, even if that agent remains unnamed. Christians, as always, draw such expectation toward the coming of Jesus who will banish all causes of fearfulness in the world of those addressed. But of course prophetic hope makes an even more elemental claim, namely, that the public process of history is not a closed system that can sustain itself forever. The upshot of that claim is that every empire (including the Assyrian empire that Micah faced) is penultimate and will pass away. It is easy to succumb to the propaganda of the dominant system and imagine that present arrangements are permanent and beyond challenge. But prophetic faith is about God-given futures that do not derive from the present system but are a new gift. It is no wonder that the ones who heard the poem might rejoice, the way the lame and outcast did in the presence of Jesus.

Isaiah 35:4–7 (Year B, Proper 18). This promissory lyric anticipates a wondrous homecoming for all those who have not the power of themselves to come home. The context is "forced migration" (exile) and the poet can see an end to such dislocation. The new presence of God in the midst of the vulnerable eradicates fear and provides energy for travel and song. The invitation is for the blind, the deaf, the lame, all those who lack clout in the old world. Beyond the vulnerable, moreover, the poem also envisions a recovery of the water supply for the animal world; one can imagine all of the animals gathering for a slow, cool long drink . . . a sign that the new creation of God has come in quite concrete ways. The new hope of the poem is that things will not stay as they have been, with fear, alienation, and deprivation. The urging of the poem is to be on the way to the new world that is breaking open by the power of God.

Isaiah 50:4–9 (Year B, Proper 19). The speaker of this poem reflects on the teaching vocation that is to instruct God's people in the demanding ways of faith. Such teaching, then as now, evoked resistance and hostility. In the face of such adversity, the teacher names the name of God... four times! Indeed, every unit of the poem begins with the divine name upon which the speaker relies. As a consequence of that divine reality, the teacher is confident about the truth-telling entrusted to him. In anticipation of Paul's argument about "justification," the speaker is confident that God "helps," so that no adversary can in fact harm him. The poem boldly imagines that the enemies will "wear out" and be "eaten up." The outcome is a word of reassurance for the hard ministry of prophetic instruction that goes against the grain of common expectation. But the teacher also recognizes that there is no alternative. This is the truth of the matter, and it must be faced.

On Meeting Denial and Death

I am not sure a sermon series on texts like these can be sustained in most conventional Christian congregations. But we have to keep trying and exploring and experimenting. Were I to try that, it would be a series on how *evangelical truth* meets our *denial* and how *evangelical hope* meets our *despair*. I have no doubt that the two pathologies of denial and despair are broad and deep in our society and provide the matrix in which we do our preaching. I think the preacher must spend some time and energy in helping people acknowledge the denial we commonly practice (not least by euphemisms) and the despair we embrace without naming it.

If that double diagnosis of our common malady can be established, even amid what will no doubt be great resistance, then the preacher can celebrate the church, the local congregation, as the only place in town where truth can be told that breaks the bubble of denial and hope can be told that shatters despair. The sermon series could seek to make the case that the church is an odd place and is and that is why we come, because we talk differently about different themes. Clearly we do so because we are in touch with ancient words (ancient bones) that are not generated by current self-deceptions. Thus the series from the randomly selected texts:

Amos 7:7-14. God's truth, as best we have access to it, is "inconvenient." The text is a model for inconvenient utterance. We are invited to play both roles, the speaker and the resister, because the topic is the ominous reality of "dislocation" (exile).

Micah 5:2-5a. This text makes a nice counterpoint to the Amos text. That text is about exposé; this text is about a new gift of leadership that can enact well-being. The coming of "messiah" for the little village makes no sense, unless it is in the context of deep dislocation, the very kind now widely known among us.

Zephaniah 3:14-20. This text builds nicely from Micah 5, and imagines the effective impact of God's good coming. The news is that every system of domination, the ones we resist and the ones from which we benefit, are quite fleeting and penultimate; we in faith wait for that beyond the system that God will give because we know that the dominant system cannot deliver on its promises to us.

Isaiah 35:4-7. This text goes further and imagines a society of compassion in which the "disabled and the vulnerable" are placed in the center of the new social vision and the new social practice that God will initiate.

Isaiah 50:4-9. This poem offers a retrospective on what hard work such teaching and preaching is. It is hard work in the church, because the church in our culture has become so "friendly" and "therapeutic" that the church unwittingly colludes with dominant culture and forms a "cocoon of pretend" that does not rush to the deep issues of power in the service of death.

Obviously such a sermon series would, in most congregations, offer ways of talking, thinking, and preaching that seem odd, intrusive, and unwelcome. Of course. That, however, is what happens when we touch the old bones and attend to the old words. Such a testimony leads, as did the ancient encounter, to "coming to life and standing up." Without such radioactive contact, there will be no "coming to life" and no "standing up." There will most often be only settling into the deathliness of denial and despair, only reclining in exhausted apathy.

Conclusion

In pondering the bones of Elisha, it becomes clear that the old prophetic legacy from a particular time and place continues to be generative. As we touch the old words, the old bones (spine) of ancient utterance, we may get energy for present utterance. We do not know what happened to the guy who touched the bones and "came to life and stood on his feet." But we may imagine that he was somebody like John Holbert. Given his new radioactive energy, he went on out to truth-telling. We may imagine that he did it effectively, like John, with grace and humor and deep caring. His name is "Legion," and John himself is a marvelous example of what happens when we touch old bones and hear old words, receiving freedom, imagination, and courage for our own proper work.

Bibliography

Erikson, Erik. "The Problem of Ego Identity." In *Identity and the Life Cycle*, 101–64. New York: International Universities Press, 1959.

Feiler, Bruce. *America's Prophet: Moses and the American Story*. New York: Morrow, 2009.

Glover, Jonathan. *Humanity: A Moral History of the Twentieth Century*. New Haven: Yale University Press 1999.

Hanson, Paul D. "Israelite Religion in the Early Postexilic Period." In *Ancient Israelite Religion: Essays in Honor of Frank Moore Cross*, edited by Patrick D. Miller Jr. et. al., 485–508. Philadelphia: Fortress, 1987.

Heschel, Abraham J. *Who Is Man?* Stanford: Stanford University Press, 1965.

King, Martin Luther, Jr. "I Have a Dream." In *Sociology of Religion: A Reader*, edited by Susanne C. Monahan et al., 404–6. Upper Saddle River, NJ: Prentice-Hall, 2001.

Westermann, Claus. *Basic Forms of Prophetic Speech*. Translated by Hugh Clayton White. Philadelphia: Westminster, 1967.

———. *Prophetic Oracles of Salvation in the Old Testament*. Translated by Keith Crim. Louisville: Westminster John Knox, 1991.

7

The Tearing of the Curtain: Matthew 27:51

I was about to fly out of Atlanta on Delta. (Out of Atlanta one flies Delta.) I was at the gate, ready to go. I was breathlessly waiting to find out whether I would be "upgraded" to "first class." I had done all the paperwork and had "qualified" for an "upgrade." It remained only to see if there was a seat available—that is, if some paying customer was a "no show," making room for me. That particular time I made it, at the last moment. Often I do not.

Comfort, Aura, and Proximity

It is, in my judgment, worth trying for an "upgrade," because the airlines are constantly making "first class" (now termed "business class") more and more comfortable, while at the same time treating "coach class" passengers in more and more neglectful and shabby ways. In first class the seats are bigger, the food is better (and sometimes it is only first class that receives a meal at all), the food is on real china with real napkins, the alcohol and movies are free. Most of all, one is "catered to," so that the ratio of flight attendants to passengers is vastly improved. They hang your coat up for you and perform all such manner of extra kindness.

    The airlines, so it appears to me, work at creating an aura about first class, an aura to match the reality. The primary vehicle for this is the curtain between the two sections of the plane. The curtain stays drawn during the flight. Partly that is done to keep "cheap fare" people out. Partly it is designed so that the people in the back of the plane cannot see how indulgently their fellow passengers are treated. And partly, I think, the curtain is there to invite the uncurbed imagination of the people in the rear, who cannot see up front, to extend in their fantasy the privileges that are in fact accorded in first class, so that the gap between the two sections is imagined to be even greater than it in fact is.[1]

The other feature of first class is that the passengers are closer to the pilot, sometimes are chatted up by an unusually friendly pilot, and may even get to peer into the cockpit. At the same time, it is clear that the cockpit is normally off limits to all passengers, first class and coach; all are kept out of the place where the real action is, where the decisions are made that determine the course of our life. Thus the plane is twice divided, by curtain and by cockpit door. The first barrier can be transgressed if one is fortunate or bold; the second is nearly inviolate. The divisions yield three quite distinct chambers, each with its clearly visible status, access, and sense of importance.

Privilege and Access

I ride Delta more than occasionally, but I am not a "professional" traveler. Rather, I am a professional Old Testament teacher. My breathless wait at the Delta gate set me to thinking. as most things do, about the Old Testament. I began to reflect upon the ancient temple in Jerusalem in relation to my wait at the gate.

The temple that Solomon built in Jerusalem was likely an imitation of a common pattern of temples in that ancient world well beyond Israel. Indeed, many of the recovered foundations of temples in the Near East are like the one described and attributed to Solomon in 1 Kings 5–8. Developed beyond the earlier unsophisticated one-room shrines, this pattern is much more developed so that it has three chambers, listed in the NRSV translation as "vestibule, nave, and inner chamber." The new, modernizing terms long ago were rendered "outer court, holy place, and holy of holies."[2] This three-part arrangement was administered in order to enact and make visible "gradations of holiness," so that each worshiper could gain access only to the appropriate chamber for which he or she was qualified by piety, religious discipline, or other socially imposed qualification.[3]

---

1. My son was recently on a non-Delta flight in which the flight attendant publicly congratulated low-fare passengers for exiting through the first-class cabin, "so you can see how it is up here."
2. See Wright, *Biblical Archaeology*, 136–40.
3. On the notions of "gradations of holiness," see Jenson, *Graded Holiness*.

The "outer court" (vestibule) was for the least qualified, perhaps women. The "holy place" (nave) was for the real worshipers, the ones who kept more rigorous religious discipline and who were characteristically men. The "inner chamber" (holy of holies) was a highly privileged place where tradition permitted only the high priest to enter, and then only once a year (see Heb 9:7). The liturgical effect (and perhaps intention?) of this arrangement was to enhance the sense of Divine Presence, to make clear that God's palpable presence was awesome and attractive, but at the same time ominous and dangerous. One did not enter into the most holy place casually, lightly, unprepared, or unqualified. While the enhancement of God's holiness was surely the first intention of the threefold arrangement, the inevitable social consequence of that arrangement was to stratify worshipers according to their access and, by implication, according to their worth.

The maintenance and distinction of these three separate zones of access to healing, forgiving, renewing holiness is accomplished by the authorization of barriers, "curtain and screen":

> You shall make a curtain of blue, purple, and crimson yarns, and of fine twisted lines; it shall be made with cherubim skillfully worked into it. You shall hang it on four pillars of acacia overlaid with gold, which have hooks of gold and rest on four bases of silver. You shall hang the curtain under the clasps, and bring the ark of the covenant in there, within the curtain; and the curtain shall separate for you the holy place from the most holy. You shall put the mercy seat on the ark of the covenant in the most holy place. You shall set the table outside the curtain, and the lamp stand on the south side of the tabernacle opposite the table; and you shall put the table on the north side. You shall make a screen for the entrance of the tent of blue, purple, and crimson years, and of fine twisted lines, embroidered with needlework. You shall make for the screen five pillars of acacia and overlay them with gold; their hooks shall be of gold, and you shall cast five bases of bronze for them. (Exod 26:31–37; cf. Heb 9:1–5)

The practical effect of the curtain is to keep people out. An additional result is to enhance what is behind the curtain so that those outside are invited to imagine even more behind the curtain than is there—more of goodness, more of awe, and more of danger, all managed by priests who are technically competent in such matters and who wear uniforms making their special authority and social status unmistakably clear to all members admitted anywhere in the holy complex. (On the uniforms, see Exod 28:1–43.)

The capacity for gradation was a serious theological issue, in part related to theological commitment and in part to ethical performance. Along with that, however, there is no doubt that some of the qualification also extended in different circumstances to race, ethnicity, gender, and, I would imagine, economic capacity. It costs a lot to go first class in any graded system of access. Thus the temple, sketched in the tabernacle of Moses (Exodus 25–31) and reported in the narrative of Solomon (1 Kings 6–7), is a three-chamber arrangement of privilege and access.

It's about Money

As I sat waiting by the Delta gate for an upgrade, I began to imagine that the "equipment" on which we were to fly (the term used by the airlines for "planes") is a social arrangement of gradation not unlike that of the ancient temple. The "equipment" has a quite parallel physical arrangement and quite similar social protocols concerning access and "upgrade."

Thus the airplane may be understood, like the temple, as a graded piece of "equipment" to get where one wants to go, or conversely, as a "mobile temple" (see Ezekiel 1). In both cases, the big deal is to "upgrade," to draw closer to the true action. In both cases, there are a lot of "coach" passengers who never qualify, but simply accept assigned seats "in the back of the temple." In both cases, moreover, a curtain is both a physical barrier and an invitation to liturgical imagination.

Since I so wanted to be upgraded (and still do), my thoughts are on those who qualify for an upgrade. They (we) are, by conventional social expectation, a "better class of people"—no screaming kids, usually well-dressed, more courteous, more patient, characteristically white, characteristically male, accustomed to privilege. The "admissions officers" who take tickets have large discretionary power. One never knows what is on the bidden computer screens, but I have heard it said that better dressed equals better qualified. In any case, being more traveled is not by itself a guarantee of closer access, though being more traveled is sometimes itself a measure how close to "holiness" one may come.

The two upgrade systems—temple and plane—seem to me deeply equivalent. While the criteria of qualification are in each case complex and variant, the ground for qualification may be merited by miles covered, etc. I cannot help but imagine, however, that in some large measure, in both cases the ground of upgrade is finally economic: "It's about money!"

Upgrades All Around

Two other notions occurred to me as I waited. First, these two ritual (sacramental) activities of upgrade—temple and plane—are interesting in and of themselves. I suggest, however, that they are more likely liturgical indications of the way in which social privilege qualifies and disqualifies people in every dimension of life—job, school, housing, health care. Everywhere there are gradations of privilege and access, and all these gradations work for legitimated taken-for-granted power arrangements of advantage. Second, the interplay of temple and airplane has led me to ponder Matt 27:51 that reports the deep, cataclysmic upheaval of Good Friday:

- At that moment the curtain of the temple was torn in two, from top to bottom (see Heb 10:6–14).
- The tearing of the curtain ends the gradations and yields equal access (see Rom 5:2; Eph 2:18; 3:12).
- We are invited to think differently about temple worship: all have equal access!
- It is mind-boggling to imagine "coach and first class" made equal.
- It is revolutionary to extend the image of equal access to housing, jobs, education, medical care, and "welfare." Perhaps it's about holiness. Maybe it's about money. Either way, it could be arranged differently. The curtain is torn: upgrades all around!

I am pleased to offer this paper in honor of Ronald Goetz, my longtime friend. He has well shepherded many matters of faith in my Alma Mater, and I am grateful.

Bibliography

Jenson, Philip Peter. *Graded Holiness: A Key to the Priestly Conception of the World.* JSOTSup 106. Sheffield: Sheffield Academic, 1982.

Wright, G. Ernest. *Biblical Archaeology.* Rev. ed. Philadelphia: Westminster, 1962.

8

Five Strong Rereadings of the Book of Isaiah

In his rich and suggestive studies of the history of modern criticism, John Rogerson has traced the primary intellectual and theological currents which have shaped our study. These include rationalism, pietism, and orthodoxy. Along with tracing these complex currents, Rogerson has inevitably cited specific instances and cases of the ways in which emerging criticism has shaped our understanding of the texts. Among others, he has exhibited the way in which the unity and single authorship of Isaiah has been critically undermined, until we have arrived at a newer critical consensus concerning the tripartite structure of the book of Isaiah and the role of the so-called Servant Songs in interpretation.

Because Rogerson's research has not reached into the later twentieth century in any sustained way, his report on critical developments in the book of Isaiah does not reach as far as the recent discussion of "canonical" Isaiah. A number of scholars, but especially Brevard Childs and Ronald Clements, have been preoccupied with showing how the critically divided book of Isaiah can be understood with canonical coherence.[1] Indeed, scholarly work on the book of Isaiah at the present time concerns the tension and relatedness between the established critical consensus and emerging attention to canonical claims.

The subject of this collection, *The Bible in Human Society*, however, sets our thinking in a quite different direction. The phrase "in human society" considers the Bible not as an object of considered reflective scholarship, but rather the use of texts in an intentional but not critically knowing way. Such use of texts may or may not be informed by scholarly opinion, but tends to use specific texts in life-contexts, without attention either to

---

1. Childs, *Introduction to the Old Testament as Scripture*, ch. 17; Clements, "The Unity of the Book of Isaiah"; and Clements, "Beyond Tradition-History."

critical consensus or canonical shape. Such texts are regularly taken up *seriatim* and freshly situated in a quite different interpretive occasions, so that the text claims for itself new meanings.[2]

Here I will identify and consider briefly five such uses. I refer to these as "strong rereadings." Readers will recognize my allusion to Harold Bloom's notion of "strong misreadings."[3] By the phrase Bloom, as I understand him, did not mean "wrong" readings, but only courageous acts of interpretation that read texts in new directions without subservience to any established or even "clear" meaning. I use the term "reread" to refer to what Bloom intends, but to suggest that the new readings, given the readers' situations, offer credible readings.

I do not suggest that such *ad hoc* readings, which may violate critical consensus or canonical intentionality, constitute any correction of or protest against more "normative" readings. But they may give us pause. They may give us pause because the more biblical texts are utilized "in human society," the less the texts are under scholarly or "canonical" constraints. If or when the use of the Bible is no longer "in human society" but only in scholarship, we shall have arrived, I suspect, at a situation when the text no longer functions with vitality. Its vitality is at the same time a measure of its public use and of the limits of scholarly or "canonical" restraints. Such a phenomenon may give us pause when we ponder the fact that the scholarly and "canonical" enterprises do not in any comprehensive way inform readings that are serious, even divergent.

Martin Luther

The first text I cite is an early text of Martin Luther. Early in his move toward his settled "Reformation" convictions, Luther participated in a "Heidelberg Dispute" on April 26, 1518, in which he first articulated his definitive "Theology of the Cross."[4] In his argument presented at the disputation, he offered forty theses, for which he then offered "proofs." From that debate

---

2. Concerning a *seriatim* approach to the texts, see Blumenthal, *Facing the Abusing God*, 47–54 and passim.

3. Bloom, *A Map of Misreading*.

4. Among the more important discussions of "the theology of the cross," see McGrath, *Luther's Theology of the Cross*; Hall, *Lighten Our Darkness*; Moltmann, *The Crucified God*.

conducted in the community of the Augustinians in Heidelberg, we will cite three theses of Luther:

19. That person does not deserve to be called a theologian who looks upon the invisible things of God as though they were clearly perceptible in those things which have actually happened (Rom 1:20).

20. He deserves to be called a theologian, however, who comprehends the visible and manifest things of God seen through suffering and the cross.

21. A theology of glory calls evil good and good evil. A theology of the cross calls the thing what it actually is.[5]

We cite theses 19 and 20 because in these central claims Luther enunciates his conviction that the "invisible things of God" are indeed hidden and not "clearly perceptible" and that the "manifest and visible things of God" are seen through "suffering and the cross."[6] In these claims, Luther's "theology of the cross" moves radically against "reason" to depend upon *revelation* and against "glory" to *suffering* as the medium and measure of God's disclosure.

But it is thesis 21 which directly concerns us. Luther here continues the sharp and dramatic antithesis in which he has begun, contrasting glory–cross, strength–weakness, wisdom–folly, good–evil. Our direct interest is that the thesis itself is an unacknowledged reference to Isa 5:20:

> Ah, you who call evil good and good evil,
> who put darkness for light and light for darkness,
> who put bitter for sweet and sweet for bitter!

In his commentary, where he is more disciplined and attentive to the text, Luther takes this "woe" to refer to the "pestilent teachers."[7] "They blaspheme and rail at it (the Word of God) but proclaim their own ungodly ideas and wisdom of the flesh, things which are never good."[8] In his commentary, Luther draws the series of woe-sayings away from the practical ordering of life to theological teaching. In his Heidelberg theses, however, he goes much further. Now the simple contrast between "good and evil" is

---

5. Grimm, ed., *Luther's Works, XXXI: Career of the Reformer I*, 52–53.
6. Ibid., 52–53, 68–69.
7. Pelikan, ed., *Luther's Works, XVI: Lectures on Isaiah, Chapters 1–39*, 65.
8. Ibid.

drawn into Luther's programmatic contrast of "glory and cross," the former being the way of the world, the latter the demanding, scandalous way of the gospel. Thus calling things by their right names is not simply faithful discernment. as an Israelite sage might have taught, but it is the submission of all discernment to the singular rule of the cross.[9]

Luther demonstrates how a particular text is by theological conviction profoundly transposed to serve an "evangelical" program. This is not to say that Luther takes the text away from Isaiah, but that he requires a rereading of Isaiah as "a theologian of the cross." The series of woes in Isa 5:8–22 and 10:1–4 now become conclusions drawn about the hiddenness of God (on which see Isa 45:15), and the judgment that the discerning eye of "natural man," that is, those not under the suffering of the cross, cannot see clearly at all. Except for the cruciality of the cross (a big exception!), this is not so far removed from Isaiah's apparent claim that the kings in Jerusalem, without faith, do not see and do not trust what God is doing in their common life.

Karl Marx

At the very beginning of his publishing career, Karl Marx wrote polemical comments on political items in the *Rheinische Zeitung*.[10] On October 25, 1842, he responded to an action of the Diet of the Rhineland that prohibited stealing firewood from enclosed land.[11] The practice of the peasants was roundly condemned by the Diet, which was of course composed of property owners who enclosed land and who granted the poor no right to take much needed wood from their property.

The one-sided and predictable action of the Diet provided an early occasion for Marx in his critique of private property and in his analysis of the law as a tool of private property. In his analysis, Marx considers the way in which an economy dominated by the propertied is separated from the realities of the social fabric in ways that are inevitably destructive.

In addition to his critique of private property and partisan law, which remained constant in his social analysis, Marx explicated a practical understanding of the poor who need wood in order to survive, and who must

---

9. For a discussion of this text in what is likely it "original" sapiential intention, see Whedbee, *Isaiah and Wisdom*, 80–110; Wolff, *Amos the Prophet*, 17–34.

10. Marx, *Texte aus der Rheinischen Zeitung*. I am grateful to Elizabeth Morgan for helping me find this text.

11. Karl Marx, "Verhandlungen des 6. rheinischen Landtags," in ibid., 78–109.

violate "law" in order to have wood. Marx asks: On what grounds are they authorized to steal? His answer is on the basis of the law or right of "custom." That is, there are old, well established social practices, long before the imposed laws of private property, which were accepted as legitimating the gathering of wood on open land. Marx's positive concern is to show that this "law of custom" is still valid, still "grounded in reason," and is the customary "right of poverty" for those who have no other recourse. Moreover, he insists that this ancient and time-honored practice belongs to the "rightful nature of things," because non-owners have rights, that is, protection accorded to the powerless.[12]

In the very life and conduct of the propertyless class, one can see a correlation between nature and poverty that creates a liveable order which cannot be violated because it is manifestly human.[13] Against the "control of the propertyless" Marx juxtaposes "the justice of the poor." In his second major move, Marx argues that this natural right has become in fact the "law of the state," which the Diet is not free to contradict. Thus in what strikes one as the reification of the state, Marx takes the true and proper function of the state as something more elemental and ultimate that these propertied law-makers cannot change when they vote merely by their own interest.

This peculiar, but characteristic, analysis of Marx brings us to the specific point of our concern. In a climactic judgment against the Diet, Marx contrasts the true concerns of the state with the frivolous and illegitimate actions of the Diet: "deine Wege sind nicht meine Wege, und deine Gedanken sind nicht meine Gedanken!"[14] It is common interpretive judgment that these words in Isa 55:8 are addressed to Judahite exiles in Babylon, asserting that repentance is the way out of exile. Informed by the study of Norman Gottwald, I have recently suggested that this assertion is a summons to embrace an intentional Judahite identity and to resist "assimilation" into the ideology of Babylonian power and Babylonian religious legitimacy.[15]

Marx of course has no interest in such historicizing. As a polemicist, he brings the text to his own urgent argument, and uses what must have

---

12. I am grateful to van Leeuwen, *Critique of Earth*, 33–65, for his suggestive discussion of Marx's discussion of the legislation of wood. On these points, see van Leeuwen, *Critique of Earth*, 43–50.

13. Ibid., 53.

14. Marx, "Debatte über das Holzdiebstahlsgesetz," 92.

15. Gottwald, "Social Class and Ideology in Isaiah 40–55"; Brueggemann, "Planned People/Planned Book?"

been powerful religious rhetoric (without acknowledging his citation of the text) to form an absolute contrast between two thoughts and two ways. The contrast is between the legitimation of what Nicholas Lash terms "reprobate materialists" and the natural right of the poor that is the law of the state. Marx, will not, of course, identify this alternative way (of the State) with the "way of Yahweh," for his opponents have already preempted theological legitimacy. The alternative way is rooted in the reality of the society, based upon reason, a mandate entrusted to the state. Thus the true state stands as a counter to this Rhineland Diet that violates right and reason, and disobeys the true mandate of the state. As in the words of Isaiah 55 against Babylon, Marx intends to legitimate those who have interests, thoughts, ways, and intentions of their own that violate this "more excellent way."

Arend van Leeuwen regards Marx's use of Isa 55:8 as altogether appropriate to the argument and not tacked on. He observes that "the spirit of the torah" is palpably evident throughout this article.[16] Thus we have a powerful rereading in Isaiah which turns the text against those who imagine they enjoy theological legitimacy for their own interests.

Three comments by way of extrapolation from Marx occur to me. First, E. P. Thompson has analyzed in some detail the practice of plebeian discourse and activity in eighteenth-century England.[17] He notes, as Marx did, that the dominant socio-economic forces have established social hegemony, and that the peasants have no court of appeal beyond "custom." Thompson comments on the interface between, on the one hand, law and ruling ideologies, and, on the other, common right usages and "customary consciousness."[18] Thompson concludes that the older custom constitutes "a moral economy" that was in profound conflict with the new "political economy."[19] It is "moral" for the same reason Marx gives. And though Thompson concludes with no such scriptural reference, his argument for England closely parallels that of Marx on the Rhineland situation.

Secondly in his programmatic study of economic history, Karl Polyani probes the enclosure laws of Speenhamland in eighteenth-century England, whereby the old peasant right of land use began to be legally prohibited.[20] Thus Marx's argument does not concern a specific Diet action only, but a

---

16. Van Leeuwen, *Critique of Earth*, 58.
17. Thompson, *Customs in Common*.
18. Ibid., 175.
19. Ibid., 258 and passim.
20. Polanyi, *The Great Transformation*.

massive, systemic shift of people and land that haunts the modern world. The practice of enclosure, now legally justified, prepares the way for modern, rapacious individualism.

Thirdly, the argument of Marx is not far distant from the programmatic notion of "God's preferential option for the poor." Of course such liberation theology is often dismissed as too much indebted to Marx. It is worth noticing that Marx's argument is a substantive one and not simply a rhetorical flourish. The sum of the argument is that, as Isaiah 55 asserts, there is more to which folk are summoned than the benefit of immediate advantage given through hegemonic control. Marx manages to make such a critical theological claim without "naming the name." Nonetheless, the words of Isaiah continue to haunt the entire social settlement upon which he reflects and which now becomes increasingly void of credibility.

Feminism

The emergence of a "feminist" hermeneutic has caused a new kind of attention to the text that raises issues related to sexual imagery and metaphor.[21] A variety of texts have been found to be pertinent to the problem of patriarchal imagery and to less exclusivist alternatives. The text that I consider, though others might be cited, is Isa 49:15–16:

> Can a woman forget her nursing child,
> > or show no compassion for the child of her womb?
> Even these may forget,
> > yet I will not forget you.
> See, I have inscribed you on thee palms of my hands;
> > your walls are continually before me.

These verses are preceded by two verses that provide a literary setting for them. In v. 13, the poet has a characteristic summons to praise, in recognition of a newness for Israel wrought by Yahweh. The reason for praise is given in the last two clauses, utilizing the term "comfort" (*nḥm*) and the verb "have compassion" (*rḥm*). This verse, however, is followed by the quotation of a communal lament, governed by the negating verbs "forsake" (*'zb*) and "forget" (*škḥ*). The stylized complaint seems to echo Lam 5:20 and was perhaps recited regularly in exile. Its function here appears to be

---

21. Extensive bibliography is offered by Day, ed., *Gender and Difference in Ancient Israel*; and, more recently, Bellis, *Helpmates, Harlots, and Heroes*.

to reject the announcement of v. 13, and to insist upon the unrelieved exilic situation of abandonment. In vv. 15–16, as is characteristic in Israel's liturgical texts, the complaint of v. 14 receives a response in the form of a divine utterance. The oracle intends to overcome the complaint, and to provide sure ground for the credibility of the assertion of v. 13. It has much interested feminist readers that in order to provide ground for the assurance, the poet must resort to maternal imagery. Here God is said to be a "mother." It is characteristic of mothers that they do not forget a suckling child or fail to "show compassion" for an infant that is their own. Of course they do not! But in an extreme case, they might! The mother who will not forget but might, and not show compassion is presented in the verses as a foil for Yahweh, who is a mother who transcends the conventional mother, who will never forget or fail to show compassion. The imagery of "mother God" is powerful and subtle. In order to make sense of the imagery, the "mother God" must be like every mother. The imagery has power because this mother God is *unlike* other mothers, for this mother God is absolute and without exception in remembering and caring for the beloved child Israel. The metaphor functions to witness to Yahweh's inexhaustible fidelity, even to an exiled Israel which imagines itself to be forgotten and forsaken.

So much is a common reading of the Isaiah texts. We may, however, notice three dimensions of feminist reading that have intensified and deepened our discernment of this text. First, early in the articulation of a feminist hermeneutic, Phyllis Trible explored, with particular attention, the uses of the term *rḥm* ("womb") in the Old Testament/Hebrew Scriptures.[22] In our text, Trible observed that the term "compassion" (*rḥm*) in vv. 13, 15, 16 makes a connection between "womb" and "compassion," and so articulates a new presence of Yahweh among the Israelites. Following Trible, this linkage has now become commonplace. But we most recognize that it was precisely the posing of a feminist question, that is, an inquiry about sexual imagery and intentionality, that evokes awareness of the rhetorical connection. Trible has daringly called attention to the "bodily reality" of Yahweh, who acts in a "womb-like" way toward beloved children who can never be forgotten.

Secondly, my former student Linda Chenowith one day in class, without excessive critical awareness but with great attentiveness to feminist issues, helped me see this text differently. She observed that if the child of v. 15 is a "suckling," the nursing mother must nurse, or she will experience

---

22. Trible, *God and the Rhetoric of Sexuality*, 31–59.

the pain of a full breast left unsucked.[23] That is, the mother remembers and shows "compassion" because the mother needs the child to suck. Thus the binding of mother and child, in the metaphor, is a bodily one giving us another dimension of bodily reality, which Trible had already seen in *rḥm*.

Thirdly, Mayer I. Gruber has taken feminist concern in a different direction.[24] He observes that Deutero-Isaiah is especially drawn to mother images for God and cites 42:14; 45:10; and 66:13, as well as other verses. Gruber is attentive to the contrast made here between mothers who forget and Yahweh who never forgets: "The Lord, who is the Mother of Israel, is not like these wicked mothers but like the good mothers."[25] Gruber's final observation, however, moves away from the intensity of the image to suggest that appeal to a mother God is a radical appeal against idolatty. He concludes: "The lesson would seem to be that a religion which seeks to convey the Teaching of God who is above and beyond both sexes caonot succeed in conveying that Teaching if it seeks to do so in a manner which implies that a positive-divine value is attached to only the one of the two sexes."[26]

Now it may be that the general intention of these observations is transparent enough in these verses, under the general rubric of "radical fidelity." If, however, we seek to go below the concept to the symbol, we must admit that the specificity and density of this particular articulation of the fidelity on God's part is uncovered for us by feminist ways of reading.[27] What feminist readers have done is to set this text in a metanarrative of feminism that is attentive to the use of images that subvert ideology and enter into density of the metaphor mostly missed in conventional reading. The notice of the "bodily" here makes us attentive to Yahweh's active, pained engagement with the child, Israel. Yahweh's stance thus is not only one of generosity or charity, but Yahweh is indeed at risk. It is then possible to return the text to the metanarrative of Scripture (and so away from any feminist metananative), but our reading will have been decisively transformed in the process of rereading.

---

23. Gruber, "The Motherhood of God," 355 n. 15, refers to Jelliffe and Jelliffe, *Human Milk in the Modern World*, with reference to the physiological issues that are pertinent.

24. Gruber, "The Motherhood of God," 351–59.

25. Ibid., 356. Mention of "good mothers" suggests reference to the defining work of D. W. Winnicott.

26. Ibid., 359.

27. Such a procedure of course appeals to the dense understanding of symbol in the work of Paul Ricoeur.

Finally, we may mention the remarkable reading of this text by Mary Gordon. Whereas current feminist reading has stressed that in this text God is like a mother, only more so, in her novel *Men and Angels* Gordon exploits the text to establish that mothers, unlike God, are quite unreliable.[28] The novel tells a tale of a series of persons, each of whom had an unreliable, if not destructive mother. This includes Anne's mother, Stephen's mother, Michael's mother, and especially Laura's mother. Indeed Laura, because of a failed family, had been driven to religion, to trust in God who is so unlike mother. Twice, Laura refers explicitly to our passage.[29] Out of this verse, she becomes an alienated, driven, almost demonic person, and in the end self-destructs.

The story is saturated with perplexed or hostile comments about mothers. Thus Jane comments:

> Mother love. I haven't the vaguest idea what it means. All these children claiming their mothers didn't love them, and all these mothers saying they'd die for their children. Even women who beat their children may they love them, they can't live without them, they wouldn't dream of giving them up. "What does it mean 'I love my child'?"[30]

Anne and Adrian have this conversation about Laura:

> Adrian: What happened to her?
>
> Anne: I don't know exactly, but I jnst feel it. She seems to unloved, so unmothered. So tremendously unhappy.
>
> Adrian: It's not your responsibility to make her happy.
>
> Anne: But she lives in my house. She takes care of my children. And if I can make her happy, I should try.
>
> Adrian: What makes you think you can?
>
> Anne: I don't know. Vanity, maybe.

---

28. Gordon, *Men and Angels*.
29. Ibid., 1, 209.
30. Ibid., 98

> Adrian: Listen, you're not her mother. You're her employer. Your responsibility is to pay her a fair wage and not to overwork her. You don't have to save her life ... You don't have to take in strays.[31]

In the end, Anne and Jane draw the conversation back to the text of Isaiah:

> Anne (of Laura's mother): That woman had said she had hated her daughter since the moment she was born. Anne thought of holding her babies, of her cheeks against their cheeks, their mouths on her breast. The woman was a monster. Motherhood was a place where hate could not enter. That was what you said, holding your baby: No one will hurt you, I will keep you from the terrible world. But that women had brought hate with her, put a knife between her breasts, pierced her child's flesh and poured in poison.[32]

> Jane: Of course it is never enough, the love of God. It is always insufficient for the human heart. It can't keep us from despair as well as the most ordinary kindness from a stranger. The love of God means nothing to a heart that is starved of human love.[33]

I cite Gordon's novel to indicate the broad range of interpretive possibilities in the text of Isaiah. Gordon has not evaded or distorted the text, but has read it from another experience, with a quite different accent. She has stayed in the field of the poem, facing the terrrible issue of God being *like* and *unlike*, but finally seeing that if not loved by those we see, being loved by one we do not see is most problematic (1 John 4:20).

James Shaver Woodsworth

The poem of Isa 65:17–25 is among the most sweeping and remarkable promissory oracles of the Old Testament. Paul Hanson and Otto Plöger have suggested that it is the voice of expectant Judaism in its period of rehabilitation after the exile that protests against a narrow, fearful Judaism.[34]

---

31. Ibid., 113.
32. Ibid., 228.
33. Ibid., 231.
34. Hanson, *The Dawn of Apocalyptic*; Plöger, *Theocracy and Eschatology*.

This text of course has often been taken out of the narrative of Judaism and situated in other narratives. I cite one poignant case of such rereading.

In the Canadian province of Manitoba, there was important labor unrest culminating the General Strike of 1919.[35] At issue in the building and metal trades were matters of collective bargaining, better wages, and lamentable working conditions. Increasing pressure was mounted about these issues through a labor movement organized as the Winnipeg Traders and Labor Council. The labor movement in western Canada was constituted in part by the import of British Socialism and included some romanticism and an important strand of Christian militarism.

On May 15, 1919, a strike called by the Traders and Labor Council prompted 30,000 workers to leave their jobs. The strikers were opposed by the Citizens Committee of 1000, composed of the monied power structure, which charged the strike was instigated by Bolsheviks and which undertook a campaign to resist any conciliation.

Our particular concern in this social emergency is the role played by James Shaver Woodsworth.[36] He had been a Christian pastor, but had left his pastorate to become directly and actively involved with the labor issues and the possibility of socialist resolutions to the political conflict and its underlying economic causes. At the pivot point of the strike, Woodsworth, among several other prominent leaders, was arrested in a vigorous police assault. Three charges of seditious libel were brought against Woodsworth. The second was:

> That J. S. Woodsworth in or about the month of June in the year of our Lord One Thousand and Nine Hundred and Nineteen at the City of Winnipeg, in the Province of Manitoba, unlawfully and seditiously published libels in the words and figures following:
>
>> Woe unto them that decree unrighteous decrees, and that write grievousness which they have prescribed, to turn aside the needy from judgment, and to take away the right from the poor of my people that widows may be their prey and that they may rob the fatherless.
>>
>> And they shall build houses and inhabit them, and they shall plant vineyards, and eat the fruit of them. They shall not build and another inhabit; they shall not plant and another eat,

---

35. See Berenson, *Confrontation at Winnipeg*.

36. See McNaught, *A Prophet in Politics*; and McCormack, *Reformers, Rebels, and Revolutionaries*, 77–97 and passim.

> for as the days of a tree are the days of my people, and mine
> elect shall long enjoy the work of their hands.[37]

The charge against Woodsworth was subsequently dropped as the monied interests prevailed and crushed the strike. For our purposes, however, it is remarkable in context that this religious-political leader of what was seen to be a social revolution is placed under arrest for, among other things, citing this ancient poetic promise from Isa 65:21–22.

That poem, in its scriptural context, of course had nothing to do with a Canadian labor conflict. It required no great interpretive ingenuity, however, to resituate those verses in the dispute between labor and monied interests, thus a usage not unlike that of Marx mentioned above. The verses of Isa 65:21–22 concern property and assert that the possession and enjoyment of property shall be safe against any usurpatious seizure. The rereading by Woodsworth was telling. It was made more so by the reaction of the anti-strike forces who in their context saw the biblical promise as a threat, because it witnessed against their rapacious economic activity. The phrasing is a libelous assertion, in the ears of those who valued an inequitable status quo and intended to protect it at all costs. A week after the arrest of Woodsworth, on June 25, the strikers returned to work. For the moment, the Isaiah text was defeated.

Beverly J. Shamana

Isaiah 43:15–21 has become in important ways a pivotal text for the book of Isaiah, and indeed for the entire Old Testament/Hebrew Bible. Gerhard von Rad has made it the hinge whereby he programmatically links the faith of Israel's torah and the prophetic literature.[38] Brevard Childs has proposed that the accent on "new things" provides a large clue to the canonical structure of the book of Isaiah, so that "old things" refers to Isaiah 1–39 and "new things" to Isaiah 40–66.[39]

---

37. Griffin, "The Influence of the Old Testament Prophets," 31–32. I am grateful to R. Gerald Hobbs for calling my attention to the case of Woodsworth, whose report to me was prompted by James Manley.

38. Von Rad, *Old Testament Theology*, vol. 2, takes Isa 43:18–19 as the opening motto for the volume. In the body of the volume be makes a great deal of the way in which Deutero-Isaiah opens a "new epoch" in the faith of Israel (e.g., 246–48, 270–71).

39. Childs, *Introduction to the Old Testament as Scripture*, 328–30. I regard Childs's suggestion, now followed by a number of scholars, as a brilliant interpretive move. It is

Our interest in this particular text, however, is of another order. The assertion of liberation rooted in God's resolve for the historical process, the governing theme of Isaiah 40–55, makes this literature peculiarly important for African-Americans who must deal theologically with the pervasive Western problem of white tyranny and specifically with the aggrieved reality of slavery in the United States. Brian Blount has reviewed in helpful detail the use of Scripture in Black preaching and the way in which texts have been found to serve this distinctive and urgent agenda.[40]

It would be easiest to cite the remarkable work of Martin Luther King Jr., who made rich and imaginative use of Scripture in his cadences of liberation.[41] The problem in citing King, of course, is that to cite his work may be to engage in a kind of "exceptionalism" about King as a most peculiar and unparalleled voice in the African-American community.

In fact, however, King's appropriation of Scripture with reference to African-American freedom is not at all exceptional but is characteristic. And therefore I cite a sermon by Beverly J. Shamana, "Letting Go," preaching on Isa 43:15-21, though in fact she focuses upon vv. 18-19:

> Remember not the former things,
>   nor consider the things of old.
> I am about to do a new thing;
>   now it springs forth, do you not perceive it?[42]

In referring to "former things," Shamana does not follow Childs in understanding this as Isaiah 1–39 (judgment), but follows the more conventional understanding that "former things" are the Exodus events, a point, against Childs, seeming clear in this text.[43] More specifically, Shamana understands the "former things" to be "let go" as the "old baggage

my judgment, however, that the older interpretation that regards the "former things" as the Mosaic events is not as easily disposed of as Childs seems to suggest. See, for example, Jer 23:7-8 as well as the allusion to Exodus in Isa 43:18-19, on which see Anderson, "Exodus Typology in Second Isaiah"; and Anderson, "Exodus and Covenant." See also the articles by Aage Bentzen and Christopher R. North referenced by Childs.

40. Blount, "Beyond the Boundaries" (see now Blount, *Cultural Interpretation*). See also Smith, *Conjuring Culture*. Smith proposes that the Bible was incessantly performative for the Black Church community in conjuring an alternative culture.

41. Cf. Washington, ed., *Testament of Hope*. More generally, see Smylie, "On Jesus, Pharaohs, and the Chosen People."

42. Shamana, "Letting Go." I am grateful to Marcia Riggs for leading me to this sermon.

43. See n. 39 above.

of slavery," or more precisely "a slave mentality."⁴⁴ The sermon is broadly based, so that it might address and appeal to many different listeners. Thus in her inventory of old things, she lists:

- parents who failed to keep promises
- a college education that promised a job
- children who fail to be grateful
- an attack of cancer, even though one is promised good health
- a failed marriage.⁴⁵

All of this is promised and has not been delivered, and so there is developed a sense of debit, of "being owed," and an acculumulation of resentment. The preacher urges that "old things are to be forgotten."

For all of this generalization, however, there runs through the sermon the primary motif of the slave mentality of ancient Israel and the parallel slave mentality of present-day African-Americans who either are free and do not accept that freedom or who refuse the summons and effort to move toward freedom not yet in hand.

Midway through the sermon, Shamana speaks of being chained to the past, and then breaks out in,

> O freedom, O freedom, O freedom over me.

She asserts, "The indomitable human and divine alliance authored by God will not stay captive, will not be fettered." And then she moves to the fuller lyric:

> And before I'd be a slave
> I'd be buried in my grave;
> And go home to my Lord and be free.⁴⁶

The sermon is concluded with the same phrasing.

Admittedly, the sermon treats freedom in a large and complex way. At the same time, however, we cannot doubt that the central issue and main current of the text is freedom for African-Americans in a residue of slavery which still continues its economic, political and emotional power to define. Shamana has taken this text from Isaiah's (and Israel's) narrative

---

44. Shamana, "Letting Go," 102.
45. Ibid., 104.
46. Ibid., 103.

of Jerusalem and has resituated it in the African-American narrative of slavery and freedom. To be sure, the two narratives are intimately paralleled, so that this is not a surprising connection to make. Yet the two larger narratives are not the same. The current tension between Jews and African-Americans in the United States may signal an important difference between the narratives, or at least a tension about who shall provide the governing interpretation, that is, "Who owns the text?"[47] Shamana, in any case, shows a compelling capacity to move the text from one narrative to another narrative without distortion, so that the ancient poem is concretely available for a new reading, and for its fresh defining power in a quite different circumstance.

Conclusion

The several usages of Isaiah I have cited evidence the ways in which Isaiah texts have been utilized in a wide variety of contexts. It is clear that these "text users" have permitted their own situations to determine the locus and intention of the text.[48] In each case, the text has been reread by being taken from the narrative of Israel's faith and its locus in the book of Isaiah, and econtextualized in a new interpretive situation of conflict.

Beyond a shared readiness to cite Isaiah, I can identify only one constant in these varied uses. In one form or another, all of these uses are in the service of protest on the side of transformation, against a status quo that resists truth "from below." Thus,

---

47. Levenson, "Exodus and Liberation," vigorously opposes "liberationist supersessionism" (157) whereby other groups, including African-Americans, preempt the Jews as the subject of Exodus liberation. He does, however, allow that Martin Luther King Jr. responsibly made use of the Israelite tradition of liberation. See the different sort of comments by Van Buren, *A Theology of the Jewish-Christian Reality. Part 2: A Christian Theology of the People Israel*, 179–83.

48. Ricoeur, "The Hermeneutical Function of Distanciation," 83, observes that when the text becomes writing, it "opens itself to an unlimited series of readings, themselves situated in different sociocultural conditions." He asserts that "the text must be able, from the sociological as well as the psychological point of view, to 'decontextualize' itself in such a way that it can be 'recontextualized.'" It is this "recontextualization" that is the subject of our study. See also Walsh, "'Leave out the Poetry': Reflections on the Teaching of Scripture." For other cases of the "recontextualization" of Isaiah, see Wheaton and Shank, *Empire and the Word*. See the reference to Isa 40:1–3 on 180 and to Isa 25:8–9 on 262. See also Miskotte, *When the Gods Are Silent*, 405–9, 415–22. Miskotte does not explicitly articulate a new context, but it is clearly implied in his eloquent testimony.

Five Strong Rereadings of the Book of Isaiah

- Luther against the church's "theology of glory"
- Marx against the political economy of the Rhineland Diet
- Feminist readers against a patriarchal reductionism that produces despair, or with Mary Gordon, against an abusive reality of distorted motherhood
- Woodsworth against an exploitative labor system, and
- Shamana against the residue of slavery.

Perhaps all of these rereaders have rightly sensed something about the radical quality of the book of Isaiah, rooted in the holiness of God and addressed to those who live "in human society."

I am pleased to offer this essay to John Rogerson, in thanks for the large ways in which be has helped us to understand ourselves more fully in the scholarly community, by attending to where we have been and how we have arrived where we are. I do so with some diffidence, for I am not sure he will regard what I have done as a legitimate enterprise.

To be sure, my approach is somewhat subjective, depending upon the happenstance of specific cases I am able to cite. My hope is to suggest in a convincing way that along with our ongoing critical work and the emerging claim of "canon criticism," we must pay attention to a third enterprise, practical usage that reflects upon the intuitive ways in which texts are understood to perform "in human society." I suggest that a study of these usages is not in conflict with more intentional critical study, but is complementary. This third enterprise, reflecting the continuing authority of the Bible as "social code," from time to time suggests hermeneutical access points to which scholarly attention must be paid.[49] The uses I have cited reflect not only a "high view" of Scripture, but also a continued valuing of the cadences and rhetoric of the text, such usage asserts the ongoing pertinence for "human society" of the One to whom these texts bear witness and through which that One becomes present.

---

49. I make reference, of course, to Frye, *The Great Code*.

Bibliography

Anderson, Bernhard W. "Exodus and Covenant in Second Isaiah and Prophetic Tradition." In *Magnalia Dei: The Mighty Acts of God: Essays on the Bible and Archaeology in Memory of G. Ernest Wright*, edited by Frank Moore Cross et al., 339–60. Garden City, NY: Doubleday, 1976.

———. "Exodus Typology in Second Isaiah." In *Israel's Prophetic Heritage: Essays in Honor of James Muilenburg*, edited by Bernhard W. Anderson and Walter Harrelson, 177–95. New York: Harper & Brothers, 1962.

Bellis, Alice Ogden. *Helpmates, Harlots, and Heroes: Women's Stories in the Hebrew Bible.* Louisville: Westminster John Knox, 1994.

Berenson, David Jay. *Confrontation at Winnipeg: Labour, Industrial Relations, and the General Strike.* Montreal: McGill-Queen's University Press, 1974.

Bloom, Harold. *A Map of Misreading.* Oxford: Oxford University Press, 1975.

Blount, Brian K. "Beyond the Boundaries: Cultural Perspective and the Interpretation of the New Testament." PhD diss., Emory University, 1992.

———. *Cultural Interpretation: Reorienting New Testament Criticism.* 1995. Reprinted, Eugene, OR: Wipf & Stock, 2004.

Blumenthal, David R. *Facing the Abusing God: A Theology of Protest.* Louisville: Westminster John Knox, 1993.

Brueggemann, Walter. "Planned People/Planned Book?" In *Writing and Reading the Scroll of Isaiah: Studies of an Interpretive Tradition*, edited by Craig C. Broyles and Craig A. Evans, 1:19–37. VTSup 70. Leiden: Brill, 1997.

Childs, Brevard S. *Introduction to the Old Testament as Scripture.* Philadelphia: Fortress, 1979.

Clements, Ronald E. "Beyond Tradition-History: Deutero-Isaianic Development of First Isaiah's Themes." *JSOT* 31 (1985) 95–113.

———. "The Unity of the Book of Isaiah." *Int* 36 (1982) 117–29.

Day, Peggy L., ed. *Gender and Difference in Ancient Israel.* Minneapolis: Fortress, 1989.

Frye, Northrop. *The Great Code: The Bible and Literature.* New York: Harcourt, Brace, 1982.

Gordon, Mary. *Men and Angels.* New York: Random House, 1985.

Gottwald, Norman K. "Social Class and Ideology in Isaiah 40–55: An Eagletonian Reading." In *The Bible and Liberation: Political and Social Hermeneutics*, edited by Norman K. Gottwald and Richard A. Horsley, 329–42. Rev. ed. Maryknoll, NY: Orbis, 1993. Reprinted in Norman K. Gottwald, *Social Justice and the Hebrew Bible*, 1:44–59. Center and Library for the Bible and Social Justice Series. Eugene, OR: Cascade Books, 2016.

Griffin, Arthur J. "The Influence of the Old Testament Prophets upon the Life and Work of James Shaver Woodsworth." PhD diss., Union Theological College, Vancouver, BC, 1951.

Grimm, Harold J., editor. *Career of the Reformer I.* Luther's Works 31. Philadelphia: Muhlenberg, 1957.

Gruber, Mayer I. "The Motherhood of God in Second Isaiah." *Revue biblique* 90 (1983) 351–59.

Hall, Douglas John. *Lighten Our Darkness: Toward an Indigenous Theology of the Cross.* Philadelphia: Westminster, 1976.

Hanson, Paul D. *The Dawn of Apocalyptic: The Historical and Sociological Roots of Jewish Apocalyptic*. Rev. ed. Philadelphia: Fortress, 1979.
Jelliffe, Derrick B., and E. F. Patrick Jelliffe. *Human Milk in the Modern World*. Oxford: Oxford University Press, 1978.
Leeuwen, Arend Th. van. *Critique of Earth: The Second Series of the Gifford Lectures Entitled 'Critique of Heaven and Earth'*. Gifford Lectures. Guildford: Lutterworth, 1974.
Levenson, Jon D. "Exodus and Liberation." In *The Hebrew Bible, the Old Testament, and Historical Criticism: Jews and Christians in Biblical Studies*, 127–59. Louisville: Westminster John Knox, 1993.
Marx, Karl. *Texte aus der Rheinischen Zeitung von 1842/43 mit Friedrich Engels' Artikeln im Anhang*. Edited by Hans Pelger. Trier: Karl-Marx-Haus, 1984.
McCormack, A. Ross. *Reformers, Rebels, and Revolutionaries: The Western Canadian Radical Movement 1899–1919*. Toronto: Uoivenity of Toronto Press, 1977.
McGrath, Alister E. *Luther's Theology of the Cross: Martin Luther's Theological Breakthrough*. Oxford: Blackwell, 1985.
McNaught, Kenneth. *A Prophet in Politics: A Biography of J. S. Woodsworth*. Toronto: University of Toronto Press, 1959.
Miskotte, Kornelis H. *When the Gods Are Silent*. Translated by John W. Doberstein. New York: Harper & Row, 1967.
Moltmann, Jürgen. *The Crucified God: The Cross of Christ as the Foundation and Criticism of Christian Theology*. Translated by R. A. Wilson and John Bowden. New York: Harper & Row, 1974.
Plöger, Otto. *Theocracy and Eschatology*. Translated by S. Rudman. Richmond: John Knox, 1968.
Polanyi, Karl. *The Great Transformation*. Boston: Beacon, 1957.
Rad, Gerhard von. *Old Testament Theology*. Vol. 2, *The Theology of Israel's Prophetic Traditions*. Translated by David M. G. Stalker. San Francisco: Harper & Row, 1965.
Ricoeur, Paul. "The Hermeneutical Function of Distanciation." In *From Text to Action*, 75–88. Translated by Kathleen Blamey and John B. Thompson. Essays in Hermeneutics 2. Evanston: Northwestern University Press, 1991.
Shamana, Beverly J. "Letting Go." In *Those Preachin' Women: Sermons by Black Women Preachers*, edited by Ellis Pearson Mitchell, 101–5. Valley Forge, PA: Judson, 1985.
Smith, Theophus H. *Conjuring Culture: Biblical Formations of Black America*. Oxford: Oxford University Press, 1994
Smylie, James H. "On Jesus, Pharaohs, and the Chosen People: Martin Luther King as Biblical Interpreter and Humanist." *Int* 24 (1970) 74–91.
Thompson, E. P. *Customs in Common*. New York: New Press, 1991.
Trible, Phyllis. *God and the Rhetoric of Sexuality*. OBT. Philadelphia: Fortress, 1978.
Van Buren, Paul M. *A Theology of the Jewish-Christian Reality*. Part 2: *A Christian Theology of the People Israel*. San Francisco: Harper & Row, 1983.
Walsh, J. P. M. "'Leave out the Poetry': Reflections on the Teaching of Scripture." In *The Struggle over the Past: Fundamentalism in the Modern World*, edited by William M. Shea, 317–26. The Annual Publication of the College Theology Society, 35, 1989.
Washington, James M., ed. *Testament of Hope: The Essential Speeches and Writings of Martin Luther King, Jr.* San Francisco: Harper, 1986.

Wheaton, Philip, and Duane Shank. *Empire and the Word: Prophetic Parallels between the Exilic Experience and Central America's Crisis*. Washington, DC: EPICA Task Force, 1988.

Whedbee, J. William. *Isaiah and Wisdom*. Nashville: Abingdon, 1971.

Wolff, Hans Walter. *Amos the Prophet: The Man and His Background*. Translated by Foster R. McCurley. Edited by John Reumann. Philadelphia: Fortress, 1973.

Acknowledgments

The author and publisher gratefully acknowledge the publications where earlier versions of these essays first appeared.

Chapter 1: "Social Criticism and Social Vision in the Deuteronomic Formula of Judges" first appeared in *Die Botschaft und die Boten: Festschrift für Hans Walter Wolff zum 70. Geburtstag*, edited by Jörg Jeremias and Lothar Perlitt, 101–14. Neukirchen-Vluyn: Neukirchener, 1981.

Chapter 2: "A Poem of Summons (Isaiah 55:1–3), a Narrative of Resistance (Daniel 1:1–21)" first appeared in *Schöpfung und Befreiung: Für Claus Westermann zum 80. Geburtstag*, edited by Rainer Albertz et al., 126–36. Stuttgart: Calwer, 1989.

Chapter 3: "Psalms 9–10: A Counter to Conventional Social Reality" first appeared in *The Bible and the Politics of Exegesis: Essays in Honor of Norman K. Gottwald on His 65th Birthday*, edited by David Jobling et al., 3–15 + 297–301. Cleveland: Pilgrim, 1991.

Chapter 4: "Prophetic Imagination towards Flourishing" first appeared in *Theology and Human Flourishing: Essays in Honor of Timothy J. Gorringe*, edited by Jeremy Law et al., 16–30. Eugene, OR: Cascade Books, 2011.

Chapter 5: "A Royal Miracle and Its *Nachleben*" first appeared in *The Economy of Salvation: Essays in Honor of M. Douglas Meeks*, edited by Jürgen Moltmann et al., 9–22. Eugene, OR: Cascade Books, 2015.

Chapter 6: "The Living Afterlife of a Dead Prophet: Words that Keep Speaking" first appeared in *Parental Guidance Advised: Adult Preaching from the Old Testament*, edited by Alyce M. McKenzie and Chales L. Aaron Jr., 123–32. St. Louis: Chalice, 2013.

Chapter 7: "The Tearing of the Curtain: Matthew 27:51" first appeared in *Faithful Witness: A Festschrift Honoring Ronald Goetz*, edited by Michael J. Bell et al., 77–83. Elmhurst, IL: Elmhurst College, 2012.

Chapter 8: "Five Strong Rereadings of the Book of Isaiah" first appeared in *The Bible in Human Society: Essays in Honour of John Rogerson*, edited by M. Daniel Carroll R. et al., 87–104. JSOTSup 200. Sheffield: Sheffield Academic, 1995.

Scripture Index

Genesis

4:10	10
18:20	10
38:7	4
38:10	4
41:1–7	74
47:13–26	55

Exodus

1:11–14	55
2	60
2:23–25	12, 39, 57
2:23	11, 75
2:27	75
3:7–9	11
3:8	12
5:4–21	55
10:29	15
11:8	15
14:10–15	11
14:10–13	12
15:25	11
16:3	14
17:4–6	14
22:22	10
25–31	97
26:31–37	96
28:1–43	96
32	5
32:10	5, 8
32:11	5
32:19	8
32:22	5

Leviticus

10:19	4
25:42	15

Numbers

11:1	5
11:10	5, 8
11:33	5
12:9	5
12:13–14	14
14:2–4	14
20:16	11
23:27	4
24:1	4
25:3	5
32:5	4, 8
32:10	5
32:12	4
32:13	4, 5, 8

Deuteronomy

4:5–8	10
7:18–19	75–76
10:21–22	76
22:24	10
22:27	11
26:7	11
29:3	76
30:11–14	10
32	1
32:30	5
32:39	2

Joshua

24:7	11
24:17	76

Judges

2:11–13	3
2:11	3
2:14	5
2:16–17	11
2:16	11
2:20	5
3:6–7	3
3:7	3
3:8	5
3:9	10, 12
3:10	17
3:12	3
3:15	12
4:1–2	6
4:1	3
4:2	5
4:3	10
6:1	3
6:6–7	10
6:7–10	7
6:8b–10	2
6:10	3
6:34	17
8:33–35	3
9:23	17
10:6–7	3
10:6	3
10:7	5
10:10–15	11
10:10–14	10, 11
10:10–12	12
10:10b–14	7
10:10	11
10:11b–14	2
10:12	11
10:14	11
10:15	11
11:29	17
12:2	12
13:25	17
14:6	17
14:19	17
15:14	17
15:19	17

1 Samuel

8:18	11
9:16	12
10:6	17
10:10	17
11:6	17
12:9	5
12:17	4
15:19	4
16:13	17
18:10	17

2 Samuel

7	22
7:14	4
11:27	4
12:9	4
13:19	10
16:14	31
24:1	5

1 Kings

2:5–9	9
2:5–6	9
2:7	9
2:8–9	9
3–11	68
4:7–19	54, 68
4:22–28	54
4:29–34	54
5–8	55
5:13–18	55
6–7	74
6:20–22	54
7:1–12	54
7:48–51	54
9:17–19	54
9:19	55
9:20–23	55
10:14–25	54
10:23–25	54

Scripture Index

10:26	54	8	73, 79–80, 85
10:28	54	8:1–6	73–77, 80
11:1–12	56	8:3	74, 76
11:3	54	8:5	76
11:14–22	56	9–10	77
11:23–25	56	9:1	83
11:26–40	56	9:2–3	72
11:31–39	61	9:3–37	73
12:1–24	56	9:6–7	72
17–19	69	9:12	72
17:1	69	10:11	73
19:19–21	69	10:18–31	73
21	69, 77	11	68
21:23	73	13	69
22	69	13:14–19	83
		13:20–21	83
2 Kings		18–20	68
2–9	69	22–23	10, 68
2	69	25:27–30	68
4–7	73	25:30	31
4	71		
4:1–7	71	**2 Chronicles**	
4:8	74	32:20–22	13
4:10–11	74		
4:22	75	**Nehemiah**	
4:25	74	5:1	10
4:27	74	9:27–28	12
4:31	75	9:27	12
4:35–36	74		
4:36	71	**Esther**	
5	71	4:1	11
5:7	72		
5:10	71	**Job**	
5:11–12	75	5:6–16	3
5:19–27	75	8:4–7	3
5:19	71	9:13–23	15
6–7	74	11:6	3
6	71, 85	11:13–20	3
6:18	71	19:7	11
6:20	71	30	14
6:21	72	32–37	42
6:22	72	35:9–12	11
6:23	71	38:1	48
6:26–27	12		
6:27	72		
8–10	73		

Psalms

9–10	35–52
9:2–19	42, 46
9:2–17	36
9:2–3	36, 38
9:2	39, 48
9:4–7	36
9:4	37
9:6	37, 39
9:7	37, 39
9:8–9	37, 40
9:8	48
9:9	41
9:10–11	41
9:10	38, 48
9:11	48
9:12	11, 39, 48
9:13–15	12
9:13	38, 39
9:14–15	40
9:14	38, 48
9:15	36, 38
9:16	37
9:17	37
9:18	37
9:19	38, 39, 40, 46, 47
9:20—10:3	46
9:20—10:2	40
9:20–21	41
9:20	47, 48
9:21	48
10	48
10:1	41, 47, 48
10:2	41
10:3–9	42, 45, 46, 48
10:3	42, 44, 48
10:4	42, 43, 44, 58
10:5–7	48
10:5	44
10:6	42, 44, 58
10:7	44
10:8	44
10:9	44
10:10–18	46
10:10–11	46, 47
10:11	46, 47, 50, 58
10:12–13	47
10:12	47, 48, 50, 58
10:13	43, 44, 58
10:14–18	48
10:14	48, 58
10:15	48, 58
10:16	48, 59
10:17–18	59
10:17	48
10:18	48
15:5	42
16:8	42
21:7	42
22:2	12
22:6	11, 12
22:22	12
30:7	42
34:4–6	59
34:7	12
34:18	11, 12
62:7	42
73:10–14	46
77:2	11
88:2	11, 12
107	39
107:6	12
107:13	12
107:19	12
107:28	12
109	37
109:13–15	37
112:6	42
142:2	11
142:6	11
145:19	12

Proverbs

8:32–36	30
10:30	42
21:13	10

Isaiah

1–39	111, 112
2:1	62, 65
3:1—4:1	63
5:7	10, 63
5:8–22	102

Scripture Index

5:8–10	63	**Jeremiah**	
5:20–23	15	6:13–15	84
5:20	101	6:13–15a	84
5:24–25	5	6:13	84
10:1–4	102	6:14	84
14:31	11	6:15b	84
15:4	11	7:1–15	55
19:20	13	8:10–12	84
25:8–9	114	11:11–12	11
35:4–7	90, 92	48:4	11
39	63	48:34	11
40–66	111	50:46	11
40–55	21, 22 30, 63	51:54	11
40	63		
40:1–3	114	**Lamentations**	
41:1–5	24	3:8	11
41:21–29	24	3:55–57	60
42:2	11	5:20	105
42:14	107		
43:15–21	111, 112	**Ezekiel**	
43:18–19	112	1	97
45:9–13	24	16:61	76
45:10	107	30:12	6
45:15	102	37:1–14	86
46	24		
46:7	11, 12	**Daniel**	
49:15–16	105	1–6	30
50:4–9	92	1	21
55	105	1:1–21	28
55:1–3	22–25, 30	1:1–2	25
55:1	22	1:3–7	25
55:2	22, 24	1:3–4	26
55:2ab	22	1:3	25
55:3	22	1:4	26
55:3b	22	1:5	26
55:8	103	1:8–17	26
56–66	21	1:9	27, 32
57:13	11	1:12	27
60–62	63	1:14–16	27
65:17–25	63–64, 86, 109	1:17	27
65:19	64	1:18–21	27
65:20	64, 86	1:20	27
65:21–22	64, 86	1:21	27
65:23	64, 86	6:8	80
65:24	64	6:15	80
65:25	64, 86	6:27	80
66:13	107		

Hosea

7:14	11
8:1–6	5
8:2	5
8:4	5
8:5	5

Joel

4:8	6

Amos

2:6	15
5:7	15
5:10–12	15
7:7–14	89, 92

Jonah

3:7–8	11

Micah

3:4	11
3:9–12	61
3:9–11	62
3:12	62
4:1–5	61–63
4:1–2	62
4:1	62
4:2	62
4:3	62
4:4	62
4:5	62
5:2–5a	89

Habakkuk

1:2	11, 12

Zephaniah

3:14–20	90

NEW TESTAMENT

Matthew

6:24	17
27:51	98

Mark

1:14–15	17
5:30	84
8:15	17

Luke

3:1–2	80
4:27	78
8:46	84
18:1–8	78
18:1	78
18:2–5	78
18:3–5	81
18:6–8	78
18:8	78
18:13	81

Romans

1:20	101
4:17	76
5:2	98

Ephesians

2:18	98
3:12	98

Hebrews

9:1–5	96
9:7	96
10:6–14	98

Revelation

21:1–5a	87

Name Index

Anderson, A. A., 36, 51
Anderson, Bernhard W., 20, 33, 112, 115, 116

Baltzer, Klaus, 30, 33
Barth, Karl, 12, 17
Begrich, Joachim, 23, 30, 33
Belenky, Mary Field, 42, 51
Bellis, Alice Ogden, 105, 116
Berenson, David Jay, 110, 116
Berger, Peter L., 4, 5, 13, 14, 17, 18
Beyerlin, Walter, 1–3, 6–7, 16, 18, 36, 40, 51
Blenkinsopp, Joseph, 21, 33
Bloom, Harold, 100, 116
Blount, Brian K., 112, 116
Blumenthal, David R., 100, 116
Boecker, Hans Jochen, 39, 51
Bowen, Murray, 37, 51
Boyce, Richard Nelson, 64, 66, 75, 82
Bream, Howard N., 19
Brodie, Thomas L., 78, 82
Broyles, Craig C., 116
Brueggemann, Walter, ix, 2, 12, 16, 18, 20, 24, 33, 37, 51, 54, 58, 66, 70, 82, 103, 116
Budick, Sanford, 33
Buss, Martin J., 50, 51
Butler, Rex, 67

Calvin, John, 23, 33,
Campbell, Edward F., Jr., 19
Cavanaugh, William T., 61, 66
Childs, Brevard S., 30, 33, 39, 51, 99, 111–12, 116
Clements, Ronald E., x, 99, 116
Clifford, Richard J., 23, 33

Crenshaw, James L., 18, 19
Croft, Steven J. L., 37, 51
Cross, Frank Moore, 16, 18, 115
Crüsemann, Frank, 36, 51

Daly, Richard J., 85
Day, Peggy L., 105, 116
de Klerk, F. W., 77
Delitzsch, Franz, 23, 33
Dietrich, Walter, 3, 18

Eissfeldt, Otto, 1, 18, 22, 33
Engelbert, Jo Ann, 36, 47, 51
Erikson, Erik, 84, 86, 93
Evans, Craig A., 116

Feiler, Bruce, 88, 93
Fishbane, Michael, 21–22, 33
Freedman, David Noel, 19
Friedman, Edwin H., 37, 51, 66
Froman, Creel, 45, 51
Frye, Northrop, 115, 116

Gammie, John G., 18, 29, 31, 33
Gaventa, John, 45, 51
Glover, Jonathan, 86, 93
Goldingay, John, 24, 33
Gordis, Robert, 8, 18, 42, 51
Gordon, Mary, 108–9, 115, 116
Gorringe, Timothy J., 53, 56, 66, 67
Gottwald, Norman K., 2, 8, 18, 24, 35, 45, 49–52, 62, 67, 103, 116
Green, Garrett, 47, 52
Griffin, Arthur J., 111, 116
Grimm, Harold J., 101, 116
Gruber, Mayer I., 107, 116

Hall, Douglas John, 100, 116
Hanson, K. C., ix, xiii, 18, 19
Hanson, Paul D., 2, 8, 18, 21, 29, 33, 86, 93, 109, 116
Harrelson, Walter, 20, 33, 116
Hartman, Geoffrey H., 33
Hedges, Chris, 81, 82
Hendel, Ronald S., 24, 33
Heschel, Abraham J., 85, 89, 93
Hobbs, R. Gerald, 111
Holbert, John, 83
Horsley, Richard A., 51, 81, 82, 116
Humphreys, W. Lee, 28, 30, 33

Jacques, Martin, 55, 67
Janssen, Enno, 10, 18
Jelliffe, Derrick B., 107, 116
Jelliffe, E. F. Patrick, 107, 116
Jenson, Philip Peter, 95, 98
Jobling, David, 24, 33, 35, 52, 66, 82
Johnson, Aubrey R., 2, 18
Johnson, Chalmers, 55, 67
Junker, H., 36, 52

Kaiser, Otto, 18
Kennedy, Paul, 41, 52
King, Martin Luther, Jr., 65–67, 87–89, 93, 112, 114, 117
Koch, Klaus, 6–7, 18–19
Kovacs, Brian W., 8, 19
Kraus, Hans-Joachim, 35, 52

LaCocque, André, 21, 30, 33
Leeuwen, Arend Th. van, 103–4, 116
Lehmann, Paul, 80, 82
Lenski, Gerhard, 45, 52
Leveen, J., 36, 52
Levenson, Jon D., 114, 117
Luckmann, Thomas, 4, 13, 18
Luther, Martin, 100–102, 115

Mandela, Nelson, 77
Manley, James, 111
Mannheim, Karl, 8, 19
Marx, Karl, 45, 102–5, 111, 115, 117
McBride, S. Dean, 17, 19
McCarthy, Dennis J., 5, 19

McCarthy, Joseph, 85
McCormack, A. Ross, 110, 117
McGrath, Alister E., 100, 117
McLellan, D., 45, 52
McNaught, Kenneth, 100, 117
Meeks, Blair, 68
Meeks, M. Douglas, 45, 52, 68
Mendenhall, George E., 2, 5, 8, 15–16, 19
Merton, Robert King, 8, 10, 13, 19
Miller, Patrick D., 18, 33, 59–60, 67, 93
Miskotte, Kornelis H., 114, 117
Mitchell, Ellis Pearson, 117
Moltmann, Jürgen, 28, 33, 68, 100, 117
Moltmann-Wendel, Elisabeth, 68
Morrison, Toni, 44 5, 49, 52
Mowinckel, Sigmund, 44, 52
Muilenburg, James, 24, 33
Murphy, Roland E., 30, 33

Neher, André, 48, 52
Neusner, Jacob, 21, 31, 34
Newman, Katherine S., 41, 52
Noth, Martin, 69, 82

Overholt, Thomas W., 13, 19

Plöger, Otto, 109, 117
Polanyi, Karl, 104, 117

Rad, Gerhard von, 2–4, 6–8, 10, 19, 21, 30, 34, 86, 111, 117
Reventlow, H. Graf, 7, 19
Richter, Wolfgang, 1, 10, 19
Ricoeur, Paul, 107, 114, 117
Riggs, Marcia, 112
Rosenberg, Daniel D., 34
Rowley, H. H., 13, 19

Sanders, James A., 34
Scharbert, J., 6, 19
Schwartz, L. S., 26, 31, 34
Scott, James C., 70, 81, 82
Seeligmann, I. L., 21, 34
Shamana, Beverly J., 111–15, 117

Name Index

Shank, Duane, 114, 117
Shea, William M., 117
Sheppard, Gerald T., 75, 82
Skinner, John, 13, 19
Smend, Rudolf, 3, 20
Smith, Theophus H., 112, 117
Smylie, James H., 112, 117
Stephens, Scott, 67

Thompson, E. P., 104, 117
Towner, W. Sibley, 28–31, 34
Trible, Phyllis, 106–7, 117
Tsevat, Mattiyahu, 48, 52
Tucker, Gene M., 34
Tutu, Desmond, 77

Van Buren, Paul M., 114, 117
Veijola, Timoo, 3, 20

Walsh, J. P. M., 114, 117

Walzer, Michael, 58, 67, 70, 82
Washington, James M., 112, 117
Welch, Joseph, 85, 89
Westermann, Claus, 12, 20, 23–25, 32, 34, 36–37, 52, 84, 86, 93
Wheaton, Philip, 114, 117
Whedbee, J. William, 102, 117
Whitelam, Keith W., 37, 52
Wijngaards, J., 16, 20
Wilder, Amos N., 47, 52, 60, 67
Willey, Patricia Tull, 63, 67
Willis, John T., 19
Wolff, Hans Walter, 1, 5, 10, 16, 20, 31, 34, 42, 52, 102, 117
Wright, G. Ernest, 1–2, 20, 95, 98
Würthwein, Ernst, 18

Yoder, John Howard, 15, 20

Žižek, Slavoj, 57, 67

www.ingramcontent.com/pod-product-compliance
Lightning Source LLC
Chambersburg PA
CBHW021935160426
43195CB00011B/1102